Evelyn Jacks'

ESSENTIAL TAX FACTS

Ace your 2008 tax return
and save money all year long

2009 EDITION

WINNIPEG, MANITOBA, CANADA

ISBN No. 978-1-897526-04-0

Printed and bound in Canada

Canadian Cataloguing in Publication Data

Jacks, Evelyn 1955-

Evelyn Jacks' essential tax facts: Ace your 2008 tax return and save money all year long – 2009 ed.

Includes Index

1. Income tax – Canada – Popular works. 2. Tax planning – Canada – Popular works. I. Title. II. Title: Essential tax facts

HJ4661.J212 2006   343.7105'2   C2006-904910-6

Published by:
Knowledge Bureau, Inc.
Box 52042 Niakwa Postal Outlet, Winnipeg, Manitoba R2M 0Z0
204-953-4769 Email: reception@knowledgebureau.com

Research and Editorial Assistance: Walter Harder and Associates and Leslie Robinson, Manager, Content Development at The Knowledge Bureau.

Cover and Page Design: Sharon Jones

CONTENTS

When you think about it, the young and the old often have so much in common—they are often in transition to or from conjugal relationships, jobs, cities, homes. They are often also primary caregivers to others. Special attention should be paid to:

Part Five—Essential Tax Facts for New Investors

So you want to be a millionaire? Then get a grip on your largest lifetime expense—your taxes—and start earning tax efficient investment income with the help of simple tax facts:

Part Six—Essential Tax Facts for Wealth Preservation

Savvy management of time and money results in powerful productivity. The tax system can really help, especially if you face funding both the university-bound and your own retirement at mid life.

INTRODUCTION

Tax season 2009 comes on the heels of the most turbulent financial times in modern history. It's hard to believe that it was the fall of 2007, when the loonie hit a modern time high of over 106.17 cents against the US dollar—the highest closing price since August of 1957. Since then the most significant financial crisis in a century has emerged, not only with global economic ramifications, but consequences for Canadian taxpayers, too.

Never have "after tax results" been more important to Canadians. A properly filed tax return, together with some basic tax planning, can provide you and your family the opportunity to increase the returns on your investments, and create new money to pay for unexpected debt, business or job losses. It can also help you reduce taxes you pay all year long, next year, and qualify for new refundable tax credits, perhaps for the first time, to increase supplemental cash flow in more difficult times.

You may wish to take some comfort in the fact that it's tax erosion, not marketplace volatility, that will eventually be your family's biggest enemy in creating and maintaining wealth. How can that be comforting? Because, while taxes are your largest lifetime expense, it is your legal right to arrange your income tax affairs within the framework of the law to pay the least possible. This is not something you can do with every type of tax—excise or GST for example. When it comes to income taxes, you do have some control over final results, but only if you take the time to learn and plan more. The purpose of this book is to help you do exactly that, in an easy-to-read format.

To avoid income taxes, and pull ahead in your own after-tax wealth management, you need to do three things:

- Reduce this year's taxes by filing tax returns to take advantage of all the deductions and credits you and your family are entitled to.

- Plan to use your tax planning options as a hedge against marketplace volatility. That is, arrange your affairs to split income with family members, defer taxes on income and even avoid tax on certain income sources entirely so that you can accumulate, grow, preserve and transition more wealth over time.

- Third, pay yourself first: don't send more money to the government than you need to. Review your tax remittances at work and/or any quarterly tax instalment payments you may be making.

It is important to expand on that last point. Employed Canadians statistically pay thousands in unnecessarily over-remitted taxes. The average tax refund for the 2007 tax year was $1400—that's close to $120 each month, loaned by you to governments, interest-free! To say the least, this is not a good investment for you, as illustrated below.

When you multiply an average annual tax refund of $1400 by the 40 or so years a typical Canadian reports taxable income from employment or self employment, the result is accumulated capital of $56,000—more than many people accumulate in their retirement savings accounts!

How much wealth could you create if that money was in your pockets instead? Plenty. When basic rules of compounding are applied to this example, it is quickly apparent how very lucrative it is to try to keep more of the money you make in your own pockets with available tax preferences and an eye to the best possible rates of return:

$1,400 INVESTED ANNUALLY FOR 40 YEARS
(30% marginal tax rate assumed)

	At 5%	At 2%
Inside registered account (example RRSP)	$177,576	$86,254
In a non-registered account	$122,513	$75,430

Source: The Knowledge Bureau's EverGreen Explanatory Notes: Retirement Income Calculator

Imagine what you could do with an extra $177,000! Real wealth is what you are left with after tax. By learning more about your tax filing rights, and actually implementing them, you can pull ahead.

In fact, the benefits of taking the time to read this book can be the most important investment you'll make this year. A good grasp of basic tax principles, together with information about recent tax changes governments have introduced, can help you:

- pay only the correct amount of tax—and not one cent more—
- qualify for greater refundable and non-refundable tax credits
- increase monthly income from social benefits, like Old Age Security and Employment Insurance.

In short, this is about tax efficiency: how to maximize your personal productivity, invest more and withdraw less from your savings when unexpected events or emergencies beyond your control occur. This year, governments have introduced several new opportunities for tax efficient savings, including

- a new "tax free" investment—the Tax-Free Savings Account (TFSA), and
- a new Registered Disability Savings Plan (RDSP).
- increased maximum dollar contribution levels for RRSP contributions
- new phased-in retirement withdrawal options from RPPs (Registered Pension Plans)
- increased contribution and withdrawal options under the RESP (Registered Education Savings Plans)

These new initiatives, and in particular the TFSA, is so important to your family's investment portfolio that it may well establish a new era in tax advantaged wealth creation for Canadian families. These new investment vehicles are introduced to you in detail later in this introduction and throughout this book.

It's your money; and it's your time. Maximize those treasures now by reviewing what's new!

ESSENTIAL TAX FACTS: THE BASICS

Whether you do it yourself or take it to a pro, a great way to approach the filing of your family's 2008 tax returns is to overview what's new in relation to the basic elements of the T1 General return—the only one that makes reference to all the lines you may have to address to file to your family's best benefit. Navigate this form by looking for:

- Page 1: Identification of the Taxpayer
- Page 2: Total Income: Lines 101 to 150
- Page 3: Net and Taxable Income: Lines 206 to 260
- Page 4: Refund or Balance Owing: Lines 420 to 486

In addition, the T1 General features Schedules 1 to 11, which provide detailed calculations for certain provisions on the return, like transfers of certain amounts between spouses and the calculation for tuition, education and textbook amounts for post-secondary students.

One schedule that all Canadians must complete is *Schedule 1: Federal Tax and Credits*. Here you will find the calculation of federal taxes payable on your income, together with a listing of all the non-refundable tax credits you will be entitled to.

Certain auxiliary tax forms may also be required to support entries on certain lines, such as Form T777 Employment Expenses claimable on Line 229 or *Form T2124 Statement of Business Activities* to support entries on Line 135.

Finally, once the federal tax return is completed, Canadians must address their provincial taxes payable. In the province of Quebec there is a separate tax return for these purposes. However, in the rest of Canada, one return is submitted, with the provincial tax calculations summarized on the federal return on two lines:

- Line 428: Provincial or territorial tax
- Line 479: Provincial or territorial tax credits

Tax changes for 2008 will now be discussed according to the income reporting profiles of taxpayers filing the T1 General tax return.

PART ONE

WHAT'S NEW?

The February 26, 2008 Federal Budget announced several important new provisions of interest to most taxpayers and their families, discussed below.

Administrative changes

Reduced Quarterly Tax Instalment Payments. Starting in 2008, the tax threshold, which is used to determine whether tax instalments are payable by individuals throughout the year, was increased from taxes owing of $2,000 to taxes owing in excess of $3,000 (this is $1,200 and $1,800 respectively for Quebec filers). Farmers and fishers, who are currently required to make one instalment payment by December 31 are not be required to make an instalment payment at all if the actual tax owing for either of the two preceding years does not exceed $3,000 ($1,800 in Quebec).

If you have been making instalment payments in 2008, review your anticipated income level for 2009 carefully. With the financial turbulence experienced since the fall of 2008, you may find that your overall income from investments, employment and business activities may have taken a hit. Commission-based financial advisors in particular may find themselves in this boat.

If this is true for you, consider requesting a reduction in your tax withholdings at work and review your quarterly instalment payment requirements. How to do this is covered in the first section of this book. This important tip alone can help you avoid selling investments at a loss to prepay taxes which may not be necessary.

New Prescribed Interest Rates. The prescribed interest rate, which is used for the purposes outlined below is set quarterly by the Canada Revenue Agency (CRA) using a formula based on treasury bill rates. Given how relatively expensive the prescribed interest rates are for delinquent taxes have been, it may make sense to pay off the tax man first before mortgages, or other debt.

	2008			
Quarter:	**1**	**2**	**3**	**4**
Prescribed interest rate on Overdue Taxes	8%	8%	7%	7%
Prescribed interest rate on Overdue Taxes	8%	8%	7%	7%
Prescribed interest rate on overdue CPP/EI premiums	8%	8%	7%	7%
Prescribed interest rate on Tax Overpayments	6%	6%	5%	5%
Prescribed rate use to compute taxable benefits, low or no- interest loans and shareholder loans	4%	4%	3%	3%

Note that the prescribed rates can be applied by spouses on loans drawn up to transfer assets legitimately from the higher earner to the lower one.

Changes for employees

At the time of writing it was widely expected that a recession in the United States could lead to potential job losses in Canada. If this might affect you, shore up your knowledge about access to benefits from your company's Registered Pension Plan (RPP). You will also want to learn more about off-setting severance packages and Employment Insurance (EI) benefits with Registered Retirement Savings Plan (RRSP) contributions. Following are recent tax changes regarding these provisions to consider in your planning:

Increased RPP Contribution Maximums. Consider ways to maximize recent contribution maximums, and "backfilling" any available contribution room based on past services provided:

	2005	2006	2007	2008	2009	2010 and thereafter
Money purchase RPPs: annual contribution limit	$18,000	$19,000	$20,000	$21,000	$22,000	indexed
Defined benefit RPPs: maximum pension benefit (per year of service)	$2,000	$2,111	$2,222	$2,333	$2,444	1/9 money limit

Phased-in Retirement Opportunities. Next, consider whether a "phased-in retirement" is the way to go in negotiating an exit clause with your employer. Taxpayers may exit their employment at age 55 on a part time basis while continuing to contribute to their RPP. This may be a good option, given market conditions.

The accumulation of pension plan benefits under a defined benefit registered pension plan may continue, starting in 2008, even if you begin receiving pension benefits, either from that plan or from another plan of the employer or someone related to the employer. You will be allowed to draw up to 60% of the benefits that have otherwise accrued under the pension plan while continuing to accumulate benefits based on current employment, provided you have reached age 55.

RRSP Contribution Maximums. You may contribute to your RRSP throughout the year and within 60 days of the new year in order to make a deduction to offset 2008 taxes. Maximum contributions are based on earned income of the immediately preceding year, as illustrated below:

Annual RRSP Contribution Dollar Limits

	2005	2006	2007	2008	2009	2010	2011
Existing	$16,500	$18,000	$19,000	$20,000	$21,000	$22,000	Indexed
Earned Income*	$91,667	$100,000	$105,556	$111,111	$116,667	$122,222	

*Prior year

Other deduction news for employees

Long Haul Truck Drivers may deduct more of their meal expenses this year as the chart below explains. Be sure to complete Form TL2 to make this deduction, and keep receipts and log books for audit purposes.

Long-Haul Truck Driver's Meals Expenses

Year	Before March 19, 2007	After March 18, 2007	2008	2009	2010	2011 & thereafter
% deductible	50%	60%	65%	70%	75%	80%

GST/HST Rebates. Employees who claim tax deductible employment expenses on Line 229 of the tax return may also qualify to claim a GST/HST Rebate on Line 457. These provisions are explained in more detail later in this book. Please be aware that the GST rate was reduced to 5% effective January 1, 2008 so the GST/HST Rebate rate available to employees who claim tax deductible employment expenses will be adjusted to 5/105 for GST and 13/113 for HST.

Northern Residents Deductions. Both the basic residency amount and the additional residency amounts available to offset high costs of living in prescribed areas in the north have increased from $7.50 per day to $8.25 per day for 2008.

Changes for pensioners and pre-retirees

Take Advantage of Pension Income Splitting. It is worth repeating that starting in 2007, pensioners have been allowed to split pension income with a spouse or common-law partner. Income that is eligible for the Pension Amount (found on line 314 of the T1) is eligible to be split. This includes income from a Registered Pension Plan, **regardless of the annuitant's age**, as well as an RRSP annuity, a DPSP annuity, a RRIF withdrawal or a locked-in RRIF withdrawal, but in these cases, only if the recipient is 65 or older.

You'll learn more about this in later chapters of the book, but for now, understand that these rules skew heavily in favor of younger employees with RPP contributions who wish to retire early. Income splitting will provide the opportunity to receive a really tax efficient return on this investment—often better than returns received on investments the marketplace as illustrated below:

A married taxpayer under age 65 will earn a $36,000 periodic pension from an RPP. The spouse does not work, is also under 65, and the couple live in Ontario. The tax savings from splitting pension income are significant in this case—over 20%! The example also contemplates a $50,000 annual superannuation:

Periodic Pension Income Amount	$36,000	$50,000
Taxes payable without income splitting	$3654	$8182
Taxes payable (split with spouse)	$2902	$6449
Savings (as a % of taxes)	$752 or 20.6%	$1,733 or 21.2%

Mutual tax recognition for pension contributions under the Canada-US Treaty. Starting in 2008 cross-border workers may deduct in their residence country, their pension contributions made in the country where they work. Cross-border commuters who contribute to a pension plan or certain retirement arrangements in the country where they work, or those who move to a new country of residence to take on short-term work assignments (up to five years) and continue to contribute to a pension plan in their first country are affected.

German Social Security. German social security benefits became taxable in Canada in 2003. For pensions which began in 2005 or earlier, the portion of the pension that is non-taxable in Canada is 50%. For pensions which begin after 2005, the percentage that is non-taxable in Canada is set in the year that the pension starts. The 50% rate for 2005 increases by 2% each year for the period 2006 to 2020 and then increases by 1% each year until the taxable percentage reaches 100%.

Clawbacks of Old Age Security and Employment Insurance. Retirees and pre-retirees should be concerned with income level in any given taxation year to stay on the right side of "clawbacks" or reductions of social benefits. The government will reduce Old Age Security and Employment Insurance (for those recently terminated from their positions, but still looking for work). For 2008 the income thresholds are the following:

Social Benefit:	Reduction Begins	Benefit Eliminated
OAS	$64,718	$105,266
EI	$51,375	Varies with EI amount

Changes for investors

There are four primary issues of concern to investors in 2009:

- The TFSA
- The RDSP
- The RESP
- Capital Loss Planning Opportunities

The New Tax-Free Savings Account (TFSA). The new Tax-Free Savings Account (TFSA) is a registered account in which investment earnings, including interest, dividends and capital gains accumulate tax free. There is no upper age limitation and no earned income qualification under this plan.

Taxpayers over the age of 17 may contribute up to $5,000 each year to such an account, or their relatives and supporting individuals may make contributions for them. The TFSA is exempt from the normal "Attribution Rules" which require higher earners who transfer or loan money to their spouses to report earnings on the transferor's return.

And, while there is no tax deduction for contributions to the account, every Canadian will accumulate "TFSA Contribution Room" each year simply by filing a tax return. That's important: do file a tax return for everyone over 17 for these purposes, as well as for eligibility for their GST Credit, an existing provision. Also know that if you forget or can't afford to make a contribution, a taxpayer's TFSA contribution room may be carried forward to the next year, allowing for a larger contribution in that year.

It gets even better: not only are earnings in the plan exempt, but withdrawals from a TFSA are not reported as income, and free up contribution room of an equivalent amount. Recipients can take the money out for whatever purpose they wish and then put the money back into the TFSA to grow when the withdrawal need is met and new savings are achieved.

Neither will any withdrawals or earnings be included in income for any income-tested benefits, such as the Canada Child Tax Benefit or Goods and Services Tax Credit. Therefore you can save and earn on a tax exempt basis while continuing to benefit from income redistribution provisions.

Therefore, planning in 2009 begins with a proactive focus on how to contribute each family member's potential $5,000 annual maximum contribution (which will be indexed in future years, by the way) to the TFSA. You will want to be sure to have the money available to do so, considering the significant potential for wealth creation with every contribution into the TFSA, as illustrated below:

1. $5,000 invested each year for a productive lifetime of 45 years (age 20 to 65) is $225,000.

2. At a 3% compounding interest rate, these TFSA savings will grow to $477,507 inside the plan, as compared to a similar investment outside the plan which would result in only $376,253. You save $101,254 more in the TFSA.

Some components of the TFSA include the following:

- **Excess Contributions.** Such contributions are subject to a 1% per month penalty until the amounts are removed.

- **TFSA Eligible Investments.** The same eligible investments as allowed within an RRSP will apply to the TFSA. A special rule will prohibit a TFSA from making an investment in any entity with which the account holder does not deal at arm's length.

- **TFSA Excluded Investments.** Prescribed excluded property for these purposes includes any obligation secured by mortgage so that individuals cannot hold their own mortgage loan as an investment in their TFSA.

- **Interest Deductibility.** Interest paid on money borrowed to invest in the TFSA is not deductible.

- **Stop Loss Rules.** A capital loss is denied when assets are disposed to a trust governed by an RRSP or RRIF. The same rule will be extended to investments disposed to a TFSA.

- **TFSA as Security.** A TFSA may be used as security for a loan or other indebtedness.

- **Departure Tax.** The TFSA is not caught by the departure tax rules by those leaving the country to become non-residents. In fact, a beneficiary under a TFSA who immigrates to or emigrates from Canada will not be treated as having disposed of their rights under a TFSA. No TSFA contribution room is earned for those years where a person is non-resident and any withdrawals while non-resident cannot be replaced. The US does not recognize the TFSA, therefore any realized income should be non-taxable when removed after emigration. However any capital appreciation will be taxable, so it may make sense to remove capital properties from the TFSA on a tax free basis immediately prior to emigrating.

- **Marriage Breakdown.** Upon breakdown of a marriage or common-law partnership, the funds from one party's TFSA may be transferred tax-free to the other party's TFSA. This will have no effect on the contribution room of either of the parties.

- **Death of a TFSA Holder.** In this case, the funds within the account may be rolled over into their spouse's TFSA or they may be withdrawn tax-free. Any amounts earned within a TSFA after the death of the taxpayer are taxable to the estate.

For more information on planning with TFSAs see **Master Your Taxes** by Evelyn Jacks.

The new Registered Disability Savings Plan (RDSP). A new saving plan designed to accumulate funds for the benefit of a disabled person was introduced in late 2008. Any person eligible to claim the Disability Amount can be the beneficiary of an RDSP and the plan can be established by them or by an authorized representative. Anyone can contribute to an RDSP – they need not be a family member. This fact has prompted many philanthropists to open accounts for the vulnerable, especially because of the wonderful opportunity to leverage individual contributions with government matches, discussed later.

Some basic components of the plan include the following:

- Contributions are not deductible, and contributors can never receive a refund of contributions.

- Investment income earned accumulates in an RDSP tax free.

- Contributions withdrawn from an RDSP are not taxable, but all other amounts – accumulated investment income, grants and bonds (discussed below) – are taxable in the hands of the beneficiary as withdrawn.

- There is no annual limit on contributions but lifetime contributions cannot exceed $200,000. Contributions are permitted until the end of the year in which the disabled beneficiary turns 59.

- The beneficiary must start to withdraw funds from the RDSP in the year he or she turns 60. Maximum annual withdrawal amounts are to be established based on life expectancies but an ability to encroach on capital is also to be provided.

- Only the beneficiary and/or the beneficiary's legal representatives can withdraw amounts from an RDSP.

As mentioned, there is a powerful opportunity to leverage individual contributions to the RDSP and make the investment even more meaningful to the recipients. A contribution to an RDSP generates two forms of direct financial assistance from government:

1. **Canada Disability Saving Grant** which will match RDSP contributions as follows:

Family Net Income

Up to $75,769*	Over $75,769*
First $500 – 300% (maximum $1,500)	First $1,000 – 100% (maximum $1,000)
Next $1,000 – 200% (maximum $2,000)	
Therefore: $1,500 contributed to RDSP generates $3,500 CDSG	**Therefore, $1,000 contributed to RDSP generates $1,000 CDSG**

*2008 levels; to be indexed annually, based on upper income limit of the 22% tax bracket

Family income is calculated in the same manner as it is for Canada Education Savings Grant purposes except that in years after the beneficiary turns 18 family income is the *income of the beneficiary* and their spouse or common-law partner. There is a lifetime maximum of $70,000 that will be funded under the CDSG and an RDSP will not qualify to receive a CDSG from the year in which the beneficiary turns **49**.

2. **Canada Disability Savings Bond.** Unlike the CDSG, there is no requirement that a contribution be made to a RDSP before a savings bond contribution is available.

The maximum annual CDSB contribution is $1,000 and is earned where family income does not exceed $21,278. The CDSB amount is phased out completely when family income is $37,885. Again, the limits are 2008 amounts and will be indexed annually. There is a lifetime maximum of $20,000 for CDSBs. Like the CDSG, CDSBs will not be paid after the beneficiary of the RDSP turns **49**.

Repayments of all CDSGs and CDSBs will be required in the ten years preceding one of the following events: (a) a withdrawal from the plan, (b) loss of eligibility for the DTC or (c) death of the beneficiary.

RDSP withdrawals will not affect any other means-tested support delivered through the income tax system including, in particular, the OAS or Employment Insurance benefits. The federal government intends to work with the provinces to ensure that the benefits of the RDSP are not eroded by a clawback of provincially provided support.

Registered Education Savings Plans (RESPS). Beginning in 2008, the period of contribution for RESP purposes is increased by 10 years. For most beneficiaries, the current limit of 21 years will be extended to 31 years. For beneficiaries eligible for the Disability Tax Credit, the 25-year contribution period will be increased to 35 years.

Likewise the deadline for termination of the plan is extended by 10 years—from the 25th anniversary of the plan to the 35th for most plans and from the 30th anniversary to the 40th anniversary for plans where the beneficiary is eligible for the Disability Tax Credit. The age limit for beneficiaries will also increase from 21 years to 31 years. Also, beneficiaries under an RESP are allowed to receive Educational Assistance Payments for up to six months after ceasing enrolment in a qualifying educational program.

- **Canada Education Savings Grants (CESG).** The maximum annual CSEG is increased from $400 for $500, so that an annual contribution of $2,500 will earn the 20% grant. Also, the ability to carry forward unused CESG room is increased from $800 to $1,000 if contributions in prior years have not earned the maximum grant. The lifetime CESG limit of $7,200 is, however, unchanged.

- **Part-Time Studies.** The existing rules limit withdrawals from an RESP to students who have at least 10 hours per week of course work. This condition will be relaxed for 2007 and subsequent years so that a student will be able to access an RESP provided they spend at least 12 hours a month on course work. Withdrawals of up to $2,500 per 13-week semester will be permitted for such students (a greater withdrawal can be obtained if approval is sought from HRDC).

Capital Loss Planning. If you were amongst many investors who crystallized losses in your non-registered portfolio in 2008, look first to use them to offset other capital gains realized for tax purposes in 2008. Then carry unabsorbed losses back to offset capital gains reported in any of the previous three years, using auxiliary form T1A Loss Carry Back. Losses remaining after this can be carried forward indefinitely to offset your future capital gains. *It is most important that you file a tax return to record and apply such losses, even if you had no capital gains this year.* The cash flow generated in tax savings from carry forward provisions may be very lucrative to you. This can help you pay down margin accounts, investment loans or take new cash back into the marketplace.

Remember that you can carry forward capital losses incurred since 1972 for the purposes of this provision. Those losses from prior years are reported on Line 253 of the T1 Return.

Capital Gains Exemption on Donation of Securities. There has been lots of good news recently on the elimination of capital gains taxes on the donation of publicly traded securities to registered charities and private foundations. The February 26, 2008 federal budget extended the current capital gains exemption on the donation of publicly-traded securities to include capital gains on the exchange of unlisted securities that are donated within 30 days of an exchange for publicly traded securities. This will include exchanges after February 26, 2008 of a partnership interest or shares in a private corporation for publicly traded shares if these shares are donated to a qualified donee within 30 days of the exchange.

Changes for business owners

Auto Logs—finally some relief from the Tax Auditor. Small business owners have more discretion in reducing their income with reasonable expenditures leading to revenue growth. However, because tax filing for business owners is based on self-assessment, there is a greater possibility a tax auditor will call. An especially thorny issue is the auto log—required by those who claim auto expenses for vehicles that have both a personal and business use component. Starting in 2009, employed commission salespeople and the self employed, who qualify to claim auto expenses, will be happy to know that a logbook maintained for "a sample period of time" instead of the full year will suffice for tax audit purposes. It's a good idea to start that sample period early in 2009.

Aligning Capital Cost Allowance (CCA) Rates with Useful Life. CCA rates are set out in the Income Tax Regulations for the purpose of allocating the right deduction for the wear and tear taxpayers suffer on the value of assets used to produce income. This is a notional deduction on the tax return, based on declining balance method of measuring depreciation. Assets are classified, and then subject to different CCA rates, which will be under review in the immediate future, to better align with the useful life of the asset, especially due to technological advancements or changes. Watch for continuing changes in classes and rates to be announced in the near future.

For 2008, the claiming of Capital Cost Allowances on various assets has changed with the most common of these being in the Manufacturing and Processing industry. A one year extension of the 50% straight line accelerated CCA for Class 29 assets was announced, as well as an additional two year period during which accelerated CCA is provided on a declining basis. Eligible assets purchased by businesses in the M & P sector in 2010 and 2011 would have two year transitional rates assigned to them. The new rules are summarized in the chart below:

Year asset purchased	First Year	Second Year	Third Year
2008	50% straight line	50% straight line	50% straight line
2009	50% straight line	50% straight line	50% straight line
2010	50% declining balance	40% declining balance	30% declining balance
2011	40% declining balance	30% declining balance	30% declining balance

In addition, there is news for small business corporations involved in mining, scientific research and exploration activities:

- **Investment Tax Credits (ITCs).** Legislation proposed in July 2008 will make the ITC carry-forward period of 20 years apply to ITCs earned in 1998 and subsequent years.

- **Flow-through mining expenditures** which qualify for the 15% ITC will include eligible expenses incurred by a corporation after March 2008 and before 2010 under a share agreement made after March 2008 and before April 2009.

- The current **Mineral Exploration Tax Credit**, which was first introduced in 2000, will be extended to flow-through share agreements entered into on or before March 31, 2009.

- In addition, a corporation's expenditure limit for **Scientific Research and Exploration & Development expenses (SR&ED)** will be determined under a new formula which will increase the maximum expenditure limit from $2 million to $3 million and increase the upper limit of the phase-out range of taxable income from $600,000 to $700,000 and increase the upper limit of the phase-out range of taxable capital employed in Canada from $15 million to $50 million. This will apply to taxation years that end on or after February 26, 2008.

Remittance of Source Deductions Relaxed. Previously, if a payroll source deduction remittance was late, the remitter was subject to a penalty equal to 10% of the amount required to be remitted, or 20% if the failure to remit is made knowingly. The penalty applied even if the remittance was only one day late. Interest was also charged on both the penalty and remittance until it is paid. The government has now implemented a graduated penalty regime that replaces the old 10% penalty. The graduated regime became effective for remittances that are due on or after February 26, 2008.

For more information on planning for small business owners see *Make Sure It's Deductible* by Evelyn Jacks.

As you can see, there is lots of news to consider in reporting income on this year's return. There are even more changes, affecting almost everyone, when it comes to tax brackets and rates and the non-refundable tax credits used to reduce tax liabilities:

New federal tax brackets and rates

A good starting point in understanding your tax liability for 2008 is a close look at tax brackets and rates. Your federal taxes are calculated based on the tax bracket your taxable income falls into. For tax year 2008, there are five brackets and rates, which have been indexed at a rate of 1.9% for inflation. For tax year 2009, the rates will remain unchanged but the brackets will be indexed by 2.5%.

2008 Brackets	2008 Rates	2009 Brackets	2009 Rates
Up to $37,885	15%	Up to $38,832	15%
$37,886 to $75,769	22%	$38,833 to $77,664	22%
$75,770 to $123,184	26%	$77,665 to $126,264	26%
Over $123,184	29%	Over $126,264	29%

Each province also has its own brackets and rates. For the most recent information see www.knowledgebureau.com/ETF for *Essential Tax Fact Sheets*.

Changes to personal amounts for all taxpayers

This year personal amounts available to families have again been indexed. A summary of the federal amounts follows. These non-refundable tax credits can be found on Schedule 1 of the federal return. Especially noteworthy are changes in 2008 for the following credits:

Medical Expenses. Certain medical expenses for the use of support animals were previously allowed only to taxpayers who are blind, deaf or have a marked restriction to the use of their arms or legs. Starting in 2008, taxpayers and/or their dependants who have severe autism or epilepsy, may claim these expenses including:

- the cost of acquiring, caring for and maintaining an animal to assist the taxpayer
- travel, board and lodging expenses for attending a school or other facility for training in the use and handling of such animals.

Other new medical expenses which qualify for this credit starting in 2008 and subsequent years:

- altered auditory feedback devices for those with speech impairments
- electrotherapy devices designed to be used by a person with a medical condition or a severe mobility impairment

- standing devices designed for those with a severe mobility impairment to undertake standing therapy
- pressure pulse therapy devices designed for use by those with balance disorders

Also, for certain drugs, medicaments or other preparations purchased after February 26, 2008, prescribed by regulation, may be claimed if purchased over the counter in cases where a pharmacist is not required to record them. This can include insulin.

Summary of personal amounts for 2007, 2008 and 2009

Personal Amounts		2007	2008	2009[3]
Basic Personal Amount	Maximum Claim[1]	$9,600	$9,600	$10,100
Age Amount	Maximum Claim[1]	$5,177	$5,276	$5,408
	Reduced by net income over[1]	$30,936	$31,524	$32,312
Spouse or Common-Law Partner Amount	Maximum Claim[1]	$9,600	$9,600	$10,100
	Reduced by net income over	$0	$0	$0
Eligible Child under 18		$2,000	$2,038	$2,089
Amount for Eligible Dependants	Maximum Claim[1]	$9,600	$9,600	$10,100
	Reduced by net income over	$0	$0	$0
Amount for Infirm Dependants	Maximum Claim[1]	$4,019	$4,095	$4,198
	Reduced by net income over[1]	$5,702	$5,811	$5,956
Pension Income Amount	Maximum Claim	$2,000	$2,000	$2,000
Adoption Expenses	Maximum Claim[1]	$10,445	$10,643	$10,909
Caregiver Amount	Maximum Claim[1]	$4,019	$4,095	$4,198
	Reduced by net income over[1]	$13,726	$13,986	$14,336
Disability Amount	Basic Amount[1]	$6,890	$7,021	$7,196
	Supplementary Amount[1]	$4,019	$4,095	$4,198
	Base Child Care Amount[1]	$2,354	$2,399	$2,459
Tuition and Education Amounts + Textbook Tax Credit[1]	Minimum Tuition	$100	$100	$100
	Full-time Education Amount (per month)	$400 +$65[2]	$400 +$65[2]	$400 +$65[2]
	Part-time Education Amount (per month)	$120 +$20[2]	$120 +$20[2]	$120 +$20[2]
Medical Expenses	3% limitation[1]	$1,926	$1,962	$2,011
Refundable Medical Expense Credit	Maximum[1]	$1,022	$1,041	$1,067
	Base Family Income[1]	$22,627	$23,057	$23,633
Canada Employment Amount	Maximum[1]	$1,000	$1,019	$1,044
Children's Fitness Tax Credit	Maximum[1]	$500	$500	$500
Credit for Public Transit Passes	Maximum	None	None	None

[1] These amounts are indexed (and some adjusted per legislation).

[2] Textbook credit

[3] Some amounts estimated based on 2.5% indexation factor.

Planning to increase non-refundable tax credits. Note that lower net income levels will help you claim more non-refundable tax credits, also known as "personal amounts". These amounts are calculated on an individual rather than family basis and reduce the taxes you otherwise must pay. Many of the credits are subject to a "clawback" or reduction, when net income levels exceed certain thresholds.

The following table shows the clawback zones for personal amounts for 2008. Proper planning, particularly with RRSP contributions for each family member with qualifying earned income can reduce the net income these amounts are based on, so that you can qualify for more tax benefits.

Clawback zones for 2008

Credit	Reduction Begins	Credit Eliminated
Age Amount	$31,524	$66,697
Spouse or Common-Law Partner Amount	$0	$9,600
Amount for Eligible Dependants	$0	$9,600
Amount for Infirm Dependants	$5,811	$9,906
Caregiver Amount	$13,986	$18,081

News for refundable tax credit recipients

Has your income changed since filing last year's return? If so, your eligibility for certain refundable tax credits may increase or decrease this year. Always monitor new benefit levels and "clawback zones"; that is, the income thresholds used to phase out your eligibility for the Working Income Tax Benefit (WITB), the Canada Child Tax Benefit (CTB), and GST Credit. Income distributed through these credits begins again in July 2009, if you file family tax returns on time and report net income (line 236 on the tax return of both spouses) within various clawback zones. Again, an RRSP contribution might help you maximize these credits, which can really help with cash flow throughout the year. This year's credits and income threshold figures are the following:

Working Income Tax Benefit	Single Taxpayer	Family or Single Parent
Minimum earned income	$3,000	$3,000
Credit rate	20%	20%
Maximum credit	$510	$1,019
Clawback begins at income of	$9,681	$14,776
Income for maximum credit	$5,550	$8,095
Maximum income before credit fully clawed back	$13,081	$21,569

Note: Rates for BC, QC and NU vary from figures in most provinces.

WITB for those with a disability. An enhanced WITB supplement will be provided for an individual (but not a dependant) who qualifies for the Disability Amount. The supplement is 20% of earned income in excess of $1,750 to a maximum of $255. This supplement is also clawed back at a rate of 15% of net income in excess of an income threshold based on whether the taxpayer is single or in a family unit.

Working Income Tax Benefit Supplement	Single Taxpayer	Family or Single Parent
Minimum earned income	$1,750	$1,750
Credit rate	20%	20%
Maximum credit	$255	$255
Clawback begins at income of	$13,077	$21,569
Income for maximum credit	$3,000	$3,000
Maximum income before credit fully clawed back	$14,777	$24,969

All benefit levels and thresholds are indexed each year. Qualifying taxpayers must apply for the credit by filing a tax return and completing Schedule 6.

Individuals can apply to have 50% their current year's estimated WITB prepaid. Prepayments will be made on the same payment cycle as GST credits are paid but the entire prepayment will be paid over the number of remaining GST payment dates remaining in the year. So, for example, an application made in April 2009 will earn 1/3rd of 50% of the estimated WITB in July, October and January. Prepayments will be reconciled to the actual entitlement when a return is filed by adding the prepayment amount to taxes owing.

Goods and Services Tax. Benefits and income thresholds increase for 2008/2009 payments:

GST Credit	July 2007 to June 2008	July 2008 to June 2009
Adult maximum	$237	$242
Child maximum	$125	$127
Single supplement	$125	$127
Phase-in threshold for the single supplement	$7,705	$7,851
Family net income at which credit begins to phase out	$30,936	$31,524

Canada Child Tax Benefit. Benefits and income thresholds also increase for 2008/2009 payments under this provision, as shown below.

The Canada Child Tax Benefit	July 2007 to June 2008	July 2008 to June 2009
Base benefit	$1,283	$1,307
Additional benefit for third child	$90	$91
Family net income at which base benefit begins to phase out	$37,178	$37,885
First child	$1,988	$2,025
Second child	$1,758	$1,792
Third child	$1,673	$1,704
Family income at which NCB begins to phase out	$20,883	$21,278
Family net income at which NCB supplement phase-out ends	$37,178	$37,885
Maximum benefit	$2,351	$2,395
Family net income at which CDB begins to phase out	$37,178	$37,885

Now that you are more aware of some of the changes that await you when filing your personal tax return, let's turn now to some issue specific planning you can consider using a tax efficient approach this year.

Top 10 things to do to create new cash in turbulent times

A purposeful approach can lead to the creation of tax efficient income and the preservation of wealth in turbulent times. Consider the following checklist; then read more about the details behind the tax savings ideas in the rest of this book.

☐ **Avoid Overpaying Tax Instalments.** Will your income be lower in 2009 than it was last year? Can you avoid making instalment payments entirely or reduce your March and June instalments which were based on income reported last year? Write the Canada Revenue Agency (CRA formerly known as Revenue Canada) a letter to do so.

☐ **Get Your Investment Priorities Right.** What comes first this year? Is it your Registered Retirement Savings Plan (RRSP) contribution? The new Tax-Free Savings Account (TFSA)? Investments in Registered Education Savings Accounts (RESPs)? Non-registered accounts? Don't know the meanings of these terms? Find out more by reading this book and talking to your tax and financial advisors.

☐ **Debt: Deductible or Not?** If you don't have a good handle on your financial condition, check it out now. Are your finances in a state of emergency or stable condition? Review your personal balance sheet and budgets and get on the right side of debt management—more assets than liabilities. If you need to manage debt, consider which loans are tax deductible and which are not? If you are sitting on excess cash be ready to do two things: pay down bad debt—non-deductible and expensive credit cards first, non-deductible mortgages next. Then invest using good (tax deductible) debt.

☐ **Pay off CRA First?** CRA charges a hefty interest rate when you owe them money. Paying them first is also a good way to avoid wage garnishees.

☐ **Know Your Tax Options When You Are in Trouble.** Deducting interest on assets with diminishing value, tax reporting consequences of foreclosures, repossessions, can either help or bite you at tax time. Get professional help if you don't know.

☐ **Margin Account Problems? Look back for relief.** The tax system is a good place to start: unfiled tax returns, errors or omissions on prior returns can lead to thousands of dollars in missed tax refunds. Remember you can go back and recover missed refunds for a period of 10 years: from tax year 1999 and forward, but that year drops off on December 31, 2009.

☐ **Create Cash with an RRSP Flip.** Don't cash in RRSPs if you can help it—that will cause a tax problem in 2009. Rather, deal with cash flow shortages by investing in an RRSP—which will create tax savings. Check out your available RRSP room. Then do an RRSP "flip"— invest existing money sitting in a non-registered savings account or Canada Savings Bond into an RRSP. That's a good way to create new cash flow with a bigger tax refund, contribute to your retirement savings and shelter investment earnings too. But there can be some traps—losses created by the flip will not be deductible. We'll tell you why later in the book.

☐ **Take Advantage of Tax Losses.** Whether you panicked and locked in losses during last year's financial crisis, or generated them as part of your year end planning strategies check out your cash flow advantages by carrying back losses to offset gains of the previous 3 hot years in the marketplace. You must file a tax return to register those losses, however.

☐ **Stress Happens—Write Off Prescriptions and Other Treatments.** Do you find yourself getting extra therapeutic massages, taking more prescription drugs? Do you know what medical expenses to write off? Expensive treatments and even travel to receive them might be possible on a tax creditable basis. Check out the many available devices, treatments and prescribed items you and your family may be able to claim.

☐ **Personal Finance 101: Plan to save more.** When mom told you to save for a rainy day, she was right, and this might be it. If you aren't positioned for six to eight months of "safety cash", now is the time to put that in place. A review of your tax position for 2009 is a good place to start in deciding how to generate new cash using tax planning and new investment vehicles to your advantage.

PART TWO

ESSENTIAL TAX FACTS FOR INDIVIDUALS AND FAMILIES

What's important

The income tax return really is the most significant financial transaction of the year for many Canadians. Over a lifetime, the annual tax bill will exceed the amounts spent on food, clothing and shelter.

Most recent federal budgets have predicted that personal tax revenues—by far the largest revenue line item for government—will increase faster than personal income growth now to the end of this decade.

This is troublesome, given recent turbulent financial markets, and the fact that Canada's primary taxpaying base is disappearing. The baby boomers are getting ready to retire—or were, that is—before the most recent financial uncertainties to plague their savings.

There is once again potential for financial crisis. Solid financial fundamentals pay off for everyone, and that's why knowing more about your after-tax affairs is critically important.

Yet, most Canadian taxpayers can't answer even basic questions about the single biggest expense of their lifetime…their family income tax bill. In this section, we will come to the rescue with answers to your essential questions about filing for Individuals and Families:

1. What is "self-assessment"?

2. Who must file a tax return?

3. What are the tax consequences of leaving Canada?

4. In what province should you file a return?

5. What is the difference between tax evasion and tax avoidance?

6. What is the tax filing deadline and penalties for missing it?

7. What's the difference between a refundable and non-refundable tax credit?

8. What are clawbacks?

9. Are all income sources taxed alike?

10. How are residents of First Nations Reserves taxed?

11. What is the significance of Net Income on the return?

12. What is the difference between your effective and marginal tax rate?

13. What income sources can be split between family members?

14. What is the definition of a dependant for tax purposes?

15. What can you do to recover from errors or omissions on the tax return?

What's new?

The February 26, 2008 Federal Budget brought in several important new provisions of interest to most taxpayers. Check out the What's New Section in Part One of this book for details:

- Quarterly Tax Instalments Thresholds Increase
- Indexing Increases Tax Brackets
- Refundable and Non-refundable Tax Credits Increase, too

Arrange to pay the correct tax... and not one cent more

It is your legal right and duty to arrange your affairs within the framework of the law to pay the least personal income taxes possible. This is legitimate tax planning. The result of properly arranging your affairs is more money in your pocket at tax time, and all year long. That's certainly worthwhile. Yet many would rather avoid CRA.

A taxpayer's relationship with the Canada Revenue Agency (CRA) is "in your face" yet conveniently deniable at the same time. With every pay cheque, a tax remittance is made on your behalf by your employer, both to ensure you prepay your taxes for the current year, and to enable you to contribute to the Canada Pension Plan (CPP) and Employment Insurance (EI) program. So, guess who gets paid first?

Unfortunately, most people also overpay their statutory deductions-tax withholding, CPP and EI premiums with every paycheque. *You get paid second, and give the government an interest-free loan at the same time.* Many self-employed or passive investors also overpay their quarterly instalment remittances.

To recover your money, you have to file a tax return... hence the annual tax filing routine. Problem is, it's really tough to be good at something you only do once a year.

This is especially true when it comes to tax, because many people feel they are required to hit a couple of moving targets: constantly changing tax laws and interpretations—often implemented retroactively—must mesh with complicated family lives and careers which are continually in flux. Yet, mastery of your tax filing position can catapult you and your family into a new financial stratosphere, especially when you pay yourself first, and most! This is not only possible, but your legal right.

Know that our tax system is based on "self-assessment"—the onus is on you to assess the income, deductions and tax credits you are entitled to. You must also file on time, or risk expensive compliance penalties. Here's how to avoid these and become a master of self assessment.

Meet your filing obligations with CRA—File a tax return

The best way to save money on your taxes over the long run is to file an audit-proof tax return, consistently and on time. Your legal obligation to the Canada Revenue Agency (CRA) is to pay only the correct amount of tax, no more and no less. Filing for some also generates an income source.

The Income Tax Act is full of special "tax preferences"—preferred taxation of certain income sources to promote economic goals, tax deductions and non-refundable tax credits, which recognize different economic circumstances of the individual and family, and refundable tax credits, which redistribute income to low and middle income earners.

Starting in 2009 there is another important reason to file: eligibility to creates contribution room for the new Tax-Free Savings Account (TFSA) for every person over the age of 17.

You can take advantage of all these tax preferences when you file a tax return. What you can't do is commit fraud or handle your tax affairs with gross negligence.

So, to begin, who must file a return? What happens if you don't? What happens if you make mistakes? How can you correct errors and omissions?

Essential TAX FACT #1

Canadian residents must report "world income" in Canadian funds.

Establish and keep your residency status

Your obligation to file a Canadian tax return rests not on citizenship, but on residency. Your Canadian residency also is what entitles you to lucrative tax deductions and refundable or non-refundable tax credits.

In today's busy world, there can be several grey areas surrounding residency for those on the go, often resulting in a case-by-case basis analysis of filing status, especially those who leave Canada temporarily. You should therefore be aware of the following definitions of residency.

- **Individual Residency.** An individual is considered to be a resident of Canada for tax purposes if they have residential ties to Canada. These taxpayers must report world income but are often eligible to claim a credit for any taxes paid to a foreign jurisdiction.

- **Deemed Residency.** Some taxpayers are considered to be residents of Canada even if they have no established residential ties. This includes individuals who:
  – Visit Canada for 183 days or more in the year
  – Work overseas as a member of the Canadian Armed Forces
  – Are a minister, high commissioner, ambassador, officer or servant of Canada
  – Perform services in a foreign country under a program of the Canadian International Development Agency
  – Are a member of the Canadian Armed Forces school staff
  – Are a spouse or dependent child of one of the above
  These taxpayers file a tax return as a normal resident.

- **Immigration and Emigration.** Those who enter the country permanently or sever all ties are considered to be "part year residents", which requires the filing of a Canadian tax return for the period of residency.

- **Non-Residency.** An individual is considered to be a non-resident of Canada if residential ties to Canada have not been established, or have been severed. These individuals may still be required to file a return in Canada if they earned income from employment or self-employment here, or have disposed of certain Taxable Canadian Property—that is property that is situated in Canada, upon which the Canadian government has reserved taxation rights.

When it comes to your taxes, it's important not to leave Canada permanently in too much of a hurry. Those who sever ties permanently must first deal with a tax reconning—a departure tax will apply to most taxable assets, based on valuation as at the date of departure. If such fair market valuation results in a capital gain, you'll need to square off with the tax department (cash or the posting of security will usually do).

**Essential
TAX FACT #2**

"Departure taxes" must be calculated if you give up your Canadian residency.

Not all properties are subject to the departure tax. Specifically excluded properties include:

- pensions and similar rights including registered retirement savings plans, registered retirement income funds, and deferred profit-sharing plans
- rights to certain benefits under employee profit sharing plans, employee benefit plans, employee trusts, and salary deferral arrangements
- in the case of those who have been resident in Canada for 5 years or less, certain qualifying property that was owned at the time the person became a resident, or was inherited since the taxpayer last became a resident of Canada
- employee stock options subject to Canadian tax
- interests in life insurance policies in Canada (other than segregated fund policies)

There are also special tax filing rules for the year you immigrate to Canada. For example, you will value assets as of the date of entry, so that you can avoid paying capital gains taxes on any value accrual that occurred before you became a Canadian resident. You will also qualify for refundable tax credits if you can establish residency here by December 31 of the tax year.

**Essential
TAX FACT #3**

Provincial taxes are based on the province of residence on December 31.

Immigrants or emigrants are considered to be "part year residents." In the year of entry or departure it's possible to be both a Canadian resident and a "part-year non-resident" for filing purposes. Accordingly, in those years, personal amounts would be prorated for the number of days of residency, and in the case of emigrants, refundable tax credits would be denied on the final return.

It is therefore wise to receive professional advice on the tax consequences of entry to or departure from Canada well in advance of your move. This can help you plan for a tax-advantaged fair market valuation date and meet all compliance requirements.

Provincial Filing Requirements. Except for the province of Quebec, which requires the filing of a separate provincial return, provincial tax calculations are included in the federal tax return through additional schedules. It is important to plan moves to less expensive provinces or from more expensive provinces wisely, as your province of residency as of December 31 determines your provincial taxes for the whole year.

Avoid tax evasion

Essential TAX FACT #4

Tax evasion is a crime... with very expensive consequences.

Tax evasion is the act of making false or deceptive statements in a return, certificate, statement or answer filed or made to the CRA in order to willfully evade or attempt to evade paying tax. Also, to participate in destroying, altering, mutilating, or otherwise disposing of the records or books of account will be considered tax evasion.

If convicted of tax evasion, besides paying the taxes, the taxpayer is liable for a fine of not less than 50% and not more than double the amount of the tax that was sought to be evaded, or imprisonment for a term not exceeding 2 years. CRA's gross negligence penalty will usually also apply to the false statement or omission of information. This amounts to 50% of tax properly payable. And of course, late filing penalties and interest could also be added if you did not file on time.

File on time

Most people dread the annual tax filing routine—it's a kind of triple negative. First, you have to spend a couple of Sundays gathering up your documentation for the whole family—that's really the hardest part. Then you have to do the return (or pay someone to do it for you). Finally, you may have to write a cheque to CRA. Unpalatable!

However, these are not reasons to ignore your tax filing obligations. The alternative is even more costly: those who owe will face late filing penalties and interest.

Remember, when you fail to file, you also set yourself up for gross negligence or tax evasion penalties, on top of the interest and late filing penalties, described below:

1. **First failure to file a return on time.** 5% of unpaid taxes plus 1% per month up to a maximum of 12 months time from the filing due date.

2. **Subsequent failure to file on time within a 3-year period.** 10% of unpaid taxes plus 2% per month to a maximum of 20 months from filing due date.

Essential TAX FACT #5

The tax filing deadline is midnight April 30 for most individuals. For the unincorporated small business owner it is June 15... but if you owe, interest will accrue from May 1 onward. So it makes sense for everyone to file by April 30.

Essential TAX FACT #6

Late filing penalties are costly, especially for repeat offenders.

Now...perhaps you have heard this line before from a delinquent filer: "I don't have to file on time—I'm getting a refund anyways!" This is complete folly! If you are tempted to put off filing a return for that reason, here are two questions to consider:

1. Why would you put yourself at risk for expensive late filing penalties if you're wrong about the refund and owe money instead?

2. Why would you continue to give the government an interest-free loan for the use of your money, which is being eroded by inflation? (Know that you won't earn any interest on balances owed to you from CRA until 30 days after you file.)

Do the simple thing and save money, too—file a tax return every year, and on time.

And there is another reason to want to file on time every year...to receive refundable tax credits throughout the year from the federal and provincial governments. This is especially true for low income earners or those who are not taxable, like single mothers, widows/ers or students. Don't miss out by failing to file a return!

Refundable tax credits don't always appear on the return

Many people don't know that the filing of a tax return under the Income Tax Act serves two purposes:

1. *As a way to reconcile taxes you paid throughout the year* either through employment source deductions or by instalment payments.

2. *As a way to meet social goals by redistributing income to low and middle income earners* with special family circumstances. This is done through the delivery of refundable federal tax credits like the Child Tax Benefit, Goods and Service Tax Credit and the new Working Income Tax Benefit, or in some provinces through provincial refundable tax credits. Families with children under age 7 may also be in receipt of Universal Child Care Benefits (UCCB), regardless of income.

Essential TAX FACT #7

Even those with little or no taxable income should file a return to receive lucrative refundable tax credits.

Statistics from the Canada Revenue Agency (CRA) report over 15 million taxable filers and over 7 million non-taxable returns filed primarily to earn *refundable tax credits*. That tells us that close to one third of Canadian tax filers understand that the tax return is an application form for lucrative credits, and that's a good thing.

Here's some more good news: you don't need to be a tax expert to benefit. Start by learning the *Basic Elements of the T1 General Return*. Use it as your "anchor document". All the lines you'll need to know about are addressed there, including income, deductions and non-refundable tax credits you may qualify for.

Take some time to get to know its five Basic Elements: Taxpayer Identification, Total Income (Line 150), Net Income (Line 236), Taxable Income (Line 260) and Non-Refundable Tax Credits (Schedule 1). These computations all lead to your refund or balance due.

Essential TAX FACT #8

Tax software—a great investment—provides a full array of most CRA forms at the tips of your fingers.

Now, pick up a tax return at your local post office and have a good look for these key lines, or even better, invest in some tax software and print out the return and its schedules. You'll also find a copy of the return in your *Essential Tax Fact Sheets* available online at www.knowledgebureau.com/ETF.

Some lucrative refundable tax credits can increase monthly cash flow—but you'll not always find their calculations on the return. To receive credits like the Canada Child Benefit and the Goods and Services Tax Credit, you and your spouse or common-law partner have to file a tax return. This is required, even if you have no income. CRA will then calculate your eligibility for credits automatically and send any qualifying amounts directly to you throughout the tax year.

Important: The value of the credits is based on combined family net income on line 236 of the tax return. This includes net income of the spouse or common-law partner. Note: an RRSP contribution, which will be discussed in more depth in later chapters, can help you reduce this number to get higher tax credits.

Now, a few more tax "secrets": You should also know that refundable credits come with accompanying "clawback zones"—income threshold levels at which your credits are reduced. Every dollar of family net income over those levels will reduce the benefits of the credits, which means that eligible low and middle income families falling within a clawback zone often pay a *higher marginal tax rate* than wealthier families.

Essential TAX FACT #9

It's good to file family tax returns together for the greatest tax benefits.

Essential TAX FACT #10

Inheritances and lottery winnings are tax exempt.

Not all income sources are subject to tax. Some income sources are tax exempt. For a complete listing of exempt income sources see *Essential Tax Fact Sheets*: visit www.knowledgebureau.com/ETF.

Two important exempt income sources are worth noting here:

Income from Personal Injury Award Property of a Minor. While the tax-payer was under 21 years of age, income derived from one or more of the following sources will be exempt:

- property received by or on behalf of a taxpayer as an award of damages in respect of the taxpayer's physical or mental injury

- property substituted for such property

- a capital gain derived from the disposition of the property or substituted property, or

- investment income that was derived from such property.

Capital gains that accrue on personal injury awards up to the date of your 21st birthday may be exempted by electing to treat any such capital property as having been disposed of on the day immediately preceding your 21st birthday for its fair market value and having been immediately re-acquired at a cost equal to those proceeds.

Income Earned on First Nations Reserves. An Indian's employment income is considered to be personal property and will usually be exempt from income tax when:

- at least 90% of the duties of an employment are performed on a reserve,
- the employer is resident on a reserve and the Indian lives on a reserve,
- more than 50% of the duties of an employment are performed on a reserve and the employer is resident on a reserve, or the Indian lives on a reserve, or
- the employer is resident on a reserve and the employer is an Indian band which has a reserve, a tribal council representing one or more Indian bands which have reserves, or an Indian organization controlled by one or more such bands or tribal councils.

When less than 90% of the duties of an employment are performed on a reserve and the employment income is not exempted by another guideline, the exemption must be prorated. The exemption will only apply to the portion of the income related to the duties performed on the reserve.

Note also that the receipt of EI benefits, retiring allowances, CPP (or QPP) payments, RPP benefits or wage loss replacement plan benefits will usually be exempt from income tax when received as a result of employment income that was exempt from tax.

Earn the most tax efficient income

Have you heard the one about the millionaire who paid no tax?

Do you have a hunch that your neighbor, who makes roughly the same gross income you do, pays less tax? Do you know why?

One of the reasons why it is difficult to compare the tax results between Canadian households with similar income levels is that income sources can be taxed differently. You and your neighbor might earn the same gross income number, but because of its source, you could be paying less tax on your income.

For example, you may be producing income from a consulting business, against which you can claim a series of business expenses like auto and home office costs. Your neighbor may work as an employee, with few tax write-offs to claim. You'll likely pay less tax.

Also, the tax system contains certain important provisions to meet economic, as well as social policy goals. Capital and business loss carry forward rules, for example, help those who take risks by providing a way to average income fluctuations. It's quite possible the millionaire who paid no tax this year lost significant sums in each of the previous 10 years and was able to use those loss carry forwards to offset taxes this year, when things came together!

The best form of income is a tax exempt one. Starting in 2009, the new Tax-Free Savings Account makes it possible to accumulate tax exempt savings throughout your lifetime, for the first time. Used together with other investment vehicles available to reduce and defer tax, average Canadians can increase their wealth by making a point to earn income that is tax-advantaged.

It is very important to diversify income sources to pay less tax overall throughout your lifetime.

One of the key wealth accumulation mistakes made by those who pay too much tax throughout their entire lifetime is that they earn income from one source only—usually employment. By diversifying your income, you can average out your tax liability, and pay less. And, when you understand how much tax the next dollar you earn attracts, it will help you arrange your efforts and your affairs towards tax efficiency.

Visit www.knowledgebureau.com/ETF to view current tax brackets and rates in Essential Tax Fact Sheets.

It should be now be apparent that the word "income" can have several different and significant meanings on the tax return, which in turn will affect your refund or balance due, and your eligibility for tax credits.

The various definitions of income on the tax return are important to note, because they will help you understand how to make income-producing decisions all year long. They can also help you with long term planning, like family income splitting. Here's an overview of the tax definitions of your income sources, so that you can plan to earn more of those which are most tax efficient:

- **Total Income (Line 150).** Includes world income from all sources including:
  - employment income
  - casual earnings or barter transactions
  - public or private pensions (possibly including some of your spouse's pension income if you elect to split it)
  - Universal Child Care Benefit (reported by lower-income spouse).
  - Investments that generate income from property like interest, dividends, rents or royalties
  - net partnership income
  - capital dispositions of assets that result in a capital gain or loss
  - employment insurance benefits
  - support, alimony or maintenance payments
  - bursaries, scholarships or fellowships received by students
  - other income-like payments for jury duty or Accumulated Income Payments from Registered Education Savings Plans
  - self-employment income
  - worker's compensation, social assistance, and federal supplements, or amounts received under the Apprenticeship Incentive Grant program (ultimately deductible and not taxable, but reported to be reflected in net income, for the purposes of calculating your tax credits)

- **Net Income (Line 236).** This number results from a series of deductions taken from Total Income on Line 150, including child care expenses, moving expenses, investment carrying charges and RRSP deductions. Use of these deductions to reduce net income is very significant, as Line 236 determines the level of social benefits paid under various programs including the Old Age Security, the federal refundable credits (Child Tax Benefit, the Working Income Tax Benefit, and the GST Credit) as well as provincial refundable credits. Net income (before including the Universal Child Care Benefit) is also the figure used to determine which spouse must report the Universal Child Care Benefits received by the family. It is also the figure used to determine whether you can claim certain amounts for dependants on your tax return. In this case, the dependants' net income level on Line 236 is used in the determination of your claim for them.

- **Family Net Income (Line 236 of both spouses' or common-law partners' returns).** This combined figure is used in the calculation of federal refundable tax credits like the Child Tax Benefit, the GST Credit and the Working Income Tax Benefit and most provincial refundable credits.

- **Taxable Income (Line 260).** This number results when further deductions are taken from Net Income on Line 236, including important items like capital losses of prior years, capital gains deductions and security options deductions. The amount on Line 260 is used to calculate federal taxes, as well as provincial taxes payable.

- **Earned Income.** This refers to income from active sources like employment and self-employment, and is used to compute RRSP, disability supports and child care deduction limits and the amount of the Working Income Tax Benefit. Note, however, that earned income definitions differ slightly for each purpose.

There is another compelling reason to understand these terms: to avoid nasty surprises at tax time—like being unable to claim child care expenses during a period of unemployment because your family failed to meet the required "earned income" levels for those purposes—or finding out that you have actually overcontributed to your RRSP because of a low "earned income" last year. Two different definitions—two very real problems...

Such misconceptions may, in fact, come home to roost on April 30. Hopefully you won't find the need to write a big cheque, instead of receiving your expected refund, all because you didn't understand tax lingo.

Control your tax bracket and marginal tax rate

In Canada, we have a progressive tax system, which means that those who have a higher taxable income during the year generally pay higher taxes. However, we have learned that the size of your tax bill can be affected by your income source as well. Tax rates are affixed to various tax brackets by two different levels of government: federal and provincial. This causes complexity for tax filers.

Federal tax rates are applied uniformly to all Canadians' taxable income and tax brackets are indexed for inflation each year. Provincial tax rates are applied to the same definition of taxable income, but tax brackets and rates are different and not always indexed for inflation.

See Essential Tax Fact Sheets at www.knowledgebureau.com/ETF for current tax brackets and rates.

It is important to understand what your effective and marginal tax rates are.

The effective tax rate is the average rate of tax paid on all income. You can find it easily by taking the taxes paid on Line 435 and dividing this number by your total income on line 150. For example:

Line 435 Total Payable	$ 11,699*
Line 150 Total Income	$ 56,393
Effective Tax Rate:	($11,699 / $56,393) = **21%**

*Subject to change based on province of residence and income mix.

Your effective tax rate takes "progressivity" into account: tax rates will rise with your income level.

The marginal tax rate is the rate of tax paid on the next dollar earned. Remember, as income increases, taxes paid are proportionately greater and benefits of tax credits can be clawed back. For example:

Current income:	$ 56, 393
Receipt of employment bonus:	$ 1,000
Taxes payable	$ 12,010
Taxes payable before bonus	$ 11,699
Difference	$ 311
Marginal Tax Rate:	**31%**

So, depending on your province of residence, you'll pay about $311 more on $1,000 of employment income for a total of 31%. This is what it costs you to earn the next like dollar.

Or, taken another way, this is how much you would save if you put that $1,000 into an RRSP. It's significant—your return on the RRSP investment is a double-digit one, from a tax point of view alone...31%!

Also know that different types of income may be subject to different marginal tax rates. (See Essential Tax Fact Sheets at www.knowledgebureau.com/ETF)

Split income, especially seniors

Because of the progressive nature of our tax structure (the more you earn the higher rate of tax you pay and the fewer refundable tax credits you are entitled to) astute taxpayers may wish to split income with family members.

But that's not so easy. There are very specific rules about income that can or cannot be split, given the attractive nature of individual tax free zones and lower tax rate on income under $37,885.

We will discuss transfer of assets in greater depth later. However, here is a list of income sources that can be "legally split" between family members:

- With spouses or common-law partners
- Wages from a business financed by the higher income earner
- Wages paid by a spouse who is required by contract of employment to hire an assistant
- Benefits from the Canada Pension Plan
- Superannuation, or other pension benefits that qualify for the pension income amount
- Taxable dividends, which can be transferred from the lower to the higher income earner if by doing so a "spousal amount" is either created or increased
- Self employment income from a proprietorship financed by the higher income earner.

Here are the new essential tax facts for splitting pension income:

"Eligible" pension income—that which can be split, prorated by the number of months in the taxation year that marriage or common-law relationship existed—is a new term which encompasses both "pension income" and "qualified pension income." This is any pension received which qualifies for the *pension income amount on Line 314*. Specifically, the split pension amount:

Essential TAX FACT #14

A person in receipt of an "eligible" pension will be allowed to split up to 50% of this income with a spouse or common-law partner.

- is deemed to be income of the transferee and
- is deductible by the transferor.

The transferee can claim the pension income amount (limited to a maximum of $2,000 a year). This has the effect of providing a "tax free zone" on the first $4,000 eligible pension income for a couple.

Residency Requirements. To qualify, both the transferee and the transferor must be resident in Canada at the end of the taxation year in which income is to be split or, in the case of a transfer in the year of death of either, at the time of death. The amount to be split must reported on an annual election form which will accompany the return of both taxpayers.

Attribution on Income from Subsequently Invested Capital. Because the split income is a tax election and not an actual payment of cash between the spouses, the normal attribution rules that would apply if cash was given for investment purposes to a lower earning spouse do not apply to split pension income.

Essential TAX FACT #15

The amount of your individual net income (Line 236) will have an effect on the size of refundable and non-refundable tax credits.

Reduce net income by increasing lucrative deductions

Your net income is a figure you should become intimately familiar with as it affects so many different areas on the return. A low net income will increase refundable and non-refundable tax credits. The best way to decrease it, by the way, is to maximize your RRSP contribution.

Take a close look at the list that follows. Net Income results from the subtraction of deductions on lines 207 to 235. Do you have any of these amounts to claim?

1. Registered Pension Plan (RPP) contributions
2. Registered Retirement Savings Plan (RRSP) contributions
3. Elected Split Pension Amount
4. Annual union or professional dues
5. Universal child care benefit repayment
6. Child care expenses
7. Disability supports deduction
8. Business investment losses
9. Moving expenses
10. Spousal support payments
11. Carrying charges and interest expenses

12. Deduction for Canada Pension Plan (CPP) contributions on self-employed earnings

13. Exploration and development expenses

14. Other employment expenses

15. Clergy residence deductions

16. Other deductions like certain legal fees or benefit repayments

17. Pension income that is reported by your spouse through pension income splitting.

Remember: A "taxable return" results when a taxable income remains after claiming allowable deductions and non-refundable tax credits.

Get a grip on non-refundable tax credits

Everyone in Canada qualifies for the Basic Personal Amount (BPA) which is $9,600 these days. This makes the first $800 or so that you earn every month tax free.

In contrast to Refundable Tax Credits, which pay a cash bonus to the tax filer even if there is little or no income and no taxes paid, non-refundable tax credits like the BPA reduce taxes payable only, and so do not help those who do not pay tax. Non-refundable tax credits can also be claimed for your dependants and are generally based on the dependant's net— not gross—income. They may be "clawed back" if income levels rise over certain thresholds.

> **Essential TAX FACT #16**
>
> Non-refundable tax credits are "tax preferences" provided to give recognition to the economic consequences of unique family circumstances.

Review Schedule 1 of your T1 General Return for a complete listing of non-refundable tax credits available for your use. Or visit www.knowledgebureau.com/ETF to view the form.

Working Income Tax Benefit: Claim it by filing a return!

The Working Income Tax Benefit (WITB) is designed to offset, in part, the high effective marginal tax rates that low income earners experience when their income increases due to the clawback of income support programs. By filing a tax return, lower earners can ease back into the workforce with the knowledge of these essential tax facts:

Essential TAX FACT #17	

Essential TAX FACT #17

The WITB is a refundable credit with a maximum credit of $510 for a single individual and $1,019 for a family (couple or single parent).

- The WITB is calculated as 20% of earned income in excess of $3,000.

- Earned income is the total of employment and business income for the year (ignoring losses).

- WITB is available to individuals without dependents earning $3,000 - $13,080 per year or a family that earns $3,000 - $21,568 per year.

- It is clawed back when net family income exceeds $9,681 (single taxpayer) or $14,776 (family or single parent).

- Net income for purposes of the clawback is calculated in exactly the same way as it is for the Universal Child Care Benefit.

- The WITB may be claimed by either spouse (or common-law partner) but only one spouse may make a claim for the family.

- Starting in 2008, families may request a pre-payment of up to one-half of their expected WITB. These payments will be issued quarterly in April, July, October and January.

File for tax benefits as a family

Modern lifestyles have brought changes to the definition of family members connected by their tax affairs. Here's what you need to know:

A spouse, for tax purposes, is someone to whom you are legally married.

A common-law partner, for tax purposes, is someone who is not your spouse but is:

- a person of the same or opposite sex with whom you lived in a relationship throughout a continuous* 12-month period, or

- someone who, at the end of the tax year, was the actual or adoptive parent of your child.

* Separations of less than 90 days do not affect the 12-month period.

Dependants. Taxpayers who support both minors or adult dependants may reap tax benefits. A dependant is generally defined as:

- a child of the taxpayer,

- the taxpayer's parent or grandparent or
- a person related to the taxpayer who is under 18 years of age or wholly dependent on the taxpayer because of mental or physical infirmity.

These qualifications need not be met throughout the year but must be met at some time during the year.

Non-Refundable Tax Credit for Children Under 18. "Where do I find a place to make a claim for my dependent children?" It may seem like one of those "stupid tax questions," (there is no such thing, by the way!), but in fact, since non-refundable tax credits replaced tax exemptions in the 1990's, there has been no place on the tax return to make a claim for children under 18. In 2008, we can now can claim a non-refundable tax credit of $2,038 for each minor child.

Essential TAX FACT #18

A non-refundable tax credit of $2,038 is available for each child under 18 at the end of the year who is the child of the taxpayer or his/her spouse or common-law partner.

The full amount of this credit can be claimed for the year including the year of birth, death or adoption. Other essential tax facts:

- Either parent may claim the credit
- Unused credits can be transferred between spouses and common-law partners.
- Where parents are estranged, the credit can be claimed only by the parent who would be eligible to claim the eligible dependant credit if that child were the parent's only child.

This credit will reduce tax at the lowest rate and is therefore of equal value to any taxpayer who owes federal tax—no matter the size of the taxpayer's income. Unused credits cannot be carried forward.

An equivalent to spouse or claim for "eligible" dependant is possible if you were single, separated, divorced, or widowed and supporting a dependant if these rules are followed:

- only one person can claim the amount for an eligible dependant in respect of the same dependant,
- no one may claim the amount for an eligible dependant if someone else is claiming the amount for spouse or common-law partner for that dependant,

- only one claim may be made for the amount for an eligible dependant for the same home,
- where more than one taxpayer qualifies to make the claim, the taxpayers must agree who will make the claim or no one will be allowed to,
- if a claim for the amount for an eligible dependant is made in respect of a dependant, no one may claim the "Amount for Infirm Dependants" or the "Caregiver Amount" in respect of the same dependant.

Some taxpayers can claim for adult dependants. If you support a dependant who is:

- at least 18 years of age, and
- dependent on you because of mental or physical infirmity

you may claim certain tax credits in respect of that dependant. To qualify, the dependant must be:

- the child or grandchild of you or your spouse or common-law partner, or
- the parent, grandparent, brother, sister, uncle, aunt, niece or nephew of you or your spouse or common-law partner and resident in Canada at any time in the year.

These definitions will help you co-ordinate tax filing requirements for the whole family—spouse or common-law partner, minor and adult dependants.

Medical expenses: Don't miss them!

Essential TAX FACT #19

If you have a loved one who must receive medical services not available in your community—treatments for cancer care are a good example—it is possible to claim travel expenses for the patient and one attendant, when that treatment is 40 kilometers or more away.

One of the most lucrative, yet most missed provisions on the tax return is the claim for medical expenses. This is discussed in detail in Part Four, however, it is worth mentioning here, as so many taxpayer are affected by extra out-of-pocket costs in this area.

Travel for medical reasons, for example, is often missed. If the taxpayer is required to travel more than 80 km from their place of residence, then claimable expenses may include hotel and meal costs.

The individual claiming travel expenses may claim similar costs for one individual accompanying the patient as long as the patient has been certified by a medical practitioner as being incapable of travelling without an attendant. Other essential tax facts:

- transportation costs include vehicle expenses including operating expenses, which consist of fuel, oil, tires, licence fees, insurance, maintenance and repairs or ownership expenses, which refer to depreciation, provincial tax and finance charges.

- You can use either the **detailed** or **simplified method** of determining reasonable meal and vehicle expenses.

Transfer family tax preferences for best benefits

One way to file family tax returns is to prepare each return separately, calculate and send each one off. That's how most people do it. This can be very costly. There are several joint, transferable or optional provisions that can be claimed on an inter-family basis. You should study these carefully:

TAX ELEMENT	PROVISION	CAN BE CLAIMED BY:
Income	–Canada Pension Plan Benefits –Taxable Dividends –Eligible pension income	–After age 60, either spouse, if an assignment of split benefits has been applied for. –Can be transferred to high earning spouse* if Spousal Amount is created or increased. –Up to 50% can be transferred to other spouse.
Deductions	–Safety Deposit Box	–Either spouse may claim if it holds household investment documents.
Non-Refundable Tax Credits	–Basic Personal Amount –Age Amount, Pension Income Amount, Disability Amount, Tuition, Education and Textbook Amounts, Amount for Dependent Minor –Claims for Spouse or Equivalent, Infirm Adults, Caregiver, Donations –Adoption Expenses –Medical Expenses –Labour Sponsored Fund Tax Credit –Amount for children born in 1990 or later –Canada Employment Amount –Public Transit Amount –Children's Fitness Amount	–Not transferable. –Transferrable to higher earner if lower earner is not taxable. In the case of the Disability Amount and Tuition, Education and Textbook amounts this can include transfers from dependants other than spouse. –Claimed by the supporting individual with higher taxable income in general. –Can be claimed by either spouse or shared between them. –Usually claimed by spouse with lower net income for best benefit. –Can be claimed by either spouse if purchased within spousal RRSP. –Can be claimed by either spouse or shared between them –Not transferable –Can be claimed by either spouse or shared between them –Can be claimed by either spouse or shared between them

*Throughout this book, spouse references include common-law partner.

Keep these transfer provisions in mind when you plan tax and investment activities throughout the year and account for them at tax time. You will be in a better position to take the information from your tax return to make some important investment and lifestyle decisions:

- How can we increase the Child Tax Benefits we receive?
- Will an RRSP help?
- Should we pay down the mortgage first?
- Should we invest the Child Tax Benefits received? In whose names?
- How can we split income between family members?
- Should we borrow more money to invest in the stock market?
- Should we consider buying life insurance or fund this with our tax savings?

Essential TAX FACT #20

It is important to know who is family for tax purposes.

Essential TAX FACT #21

Families make economic decisions as a unit; when you prepare taxes as a family unit, you'll get the best tax benefits.

As you can see, the benefits of looking at your tax filing activities from a family point of view will influence your wealth accumulation activities and inter-generational estate planning. The family that files together, saves more money together.

Recovering gold on prior filed returns

It may be too good to be true…if you learn something new in reading this book and find that you have missed lucrative tax provisions on prior tax returns, you may be able to recover tax gold by adjusting those prior filed returns. To do so, you'll want to keep your Notice of Assessment or Reassessment, which you'll receive with your refund cheque or balance due after filing your return, in a safe place, to grab important information you need to manage your tax affairs over time.

The Income Tax Act contains a definition of a "normal reassessment period", which is often referred to as the "statute of limitations" since it limits CRA's ability to reassess any tax year to the period that ends three years after the mailing of the original Notice of Assessment or Reassessment for the tax year, except in the case of fraud, in which case, there is no time limit. You can avoid gross negligence or tax evasion penalties by voluntarily complying with the law to correct errors or omissions.

Taxpayers, however, can request adjustments to prior filed returns within ten years after the end of the taxation year being adjusted.

This is a great way to recover "gold" from prior years. Many taxpayers miss claiming all the deductions and credits they are entitled to.

Here's how to adjust your return:

- If you think you missed claiming something on a prior filed return, call your tax practitioner to make an adjustment or do it yourself using form T1-ADJ, available on the CRA's website.

- Have supporting documentation available in case of audit.

- Never file a second tax return.

Taxpayer Relief Provisions—know that interest and late filing penalties may be avoided in hardship cases—like illness, death of a family member or other factors beyond your control. It pays to have been a "model taxpayer" when situations like this arise. Simply write a letter to the Fairness Committee at your local CRA tax services office.

**CHAPTER REFLECTION:
TAX PLANNING TIPS FOR INDIVIDUALS AND FAMILIES**

Filing a tax return is about last year. Study your final tax results carefully. In reconciling income, deductions, credits and tax payable for last year, compute your effective tax rate for the current year, contemplate what your marginal tax rate is for future income sources. Then plan to take advantage of all tax preferences you are entitled to. You'll want to:

1. Arrange your affairs, within the framework of the law, to pay the least taxes. So make it your business to know more about your tax filing rights.

2. Report "world income" in Canadian funds.

3. Anticipate "departure taxes" if you give up your residency.

4. Know that provincial tax rates are based on your province of residence on December 31.

5. Avoid the crime of tax evasion…which comes with very expensive consequences.

6. Avoid costly late filing penalties: file by midnight April 30.

7. File even if you have little or no taxable income to take advantage of lucrative refundable tax credits.

8. Invest in tax software to get forms and "what if" scenarios at your fingertips.

9. File family returns together for best tax results.

10. Start with the lowest income earner first to maximize transferable provisions.

11. Understand that not all income sources are taxed alike.

12. Plan to earn income from tax exempt sources.

13. Split income among family members where possible.

14. Beef up claims for refundable and non-refundable tax credits.

15. Adjust errors or omissions on prior filed returns within ten years.

16. Take advantage of taxpayer relief provisions.

NOW PUT MORE MONEY IN YOUR POCKET ALL YEAR LONG…

PERSPECTIVE

- Every month in which tax is overpaid to the government is a month it doesn't work for you. This is robbing you of the time value of money.

- Pay yourself first by increasing tax deductions and credits you are entitled to.

- Paying tax penalties is just not smart—always file a return on time.

- Take a new approach—take control of your after-tax results.

- Get ready for real fun—tax planning all year long can really pay off over your lifetime.

PART THREE

ESSENTIAL TAX FACTS
FOR EMPLOYEES

What's important?

"Mine is just a simple tax return." How often you have heard taxpayers with T4 slips say just that? It's just one slip, they think, but in reality, Line 101—employment income—links up with more lines throughout the tax return than any other. That means you have the potential to miss more deductions and tax credits than others.

Add to that the fact that the majority of Canadians—about 15 million—earn their income from precisely that source…you have a recipe for over-payment of tax. That's because your employer is required to withhold and submit your taxes on your behalf. What you see is not your gross but your net income, after taxes.

The good news is that you likely will be able to recover some of that by filing a return. The average Canadian overpays his taxes by about $120 a month—enough to start an education, investment or retirement savings plan.

Try to answer the following questions about filing a return for an employee. Then read on to find out more about the Essential Tax Facts those who are employed:

1. What is the definition of a tax refund?

2. When are you considered to be employed for tax purposes?

3. Who can claim the Canada Employment Credit and how much is it?

4. Why should you submit *Form TD1 Tax Credit Return* to your employer?

5. How can you reduce the taxes your employer withholds from your paycheque?

6. What is a salary deferral arrangement?

7. What tax free and taxable benefits do you want to receive from your employer?

8. What is a wage loss replacement plan and how are benefits received taxed?

9. How much can you deduct when you contribute to an employer-sponsored pension plan?

10. How will the stock options your employer gives you be taxed on your return?

11. What are the new rules for claiming board and lodging expenses of truckers?

12. What out-of-pocket expenses paid by the employee can be deducted on the return?

13. Do you have to report the monthly auto allowance your employer gives you?

14. How do you calculate the write off for home office expenses?

15. What can be claimed as moving expenses when you accept a job in another province?

What's new?

Check out Part One of this book and this chapter for details on the following tax changes for employees this tax year:

- Increased RPP and RRSP Contribution Maximums
- New Phased-in Retirement Opportunities for RPP Contributors
- Increased Meal Claims for Long Haul Truck Drivers
- Increased GST/HST Rebates
- Increased Northern Residents Deductions

Repeat after me: "A tax refund is a bad thing…"

Did you know that the average tax refund in Canada is over $1,440? The vast majority of Canadians overpay their taxes at tax time and all year long, to the tune of $120 a month. Why is this?

One reason is that if you are an employee, you are not the first person who gets paid for your work. Your income tax deductions come right off the top and are remitted to the government for you. You don't see it, you rarely understand how much it is, and you are likely overpaying your obligations every month…a fact when you get a tax refund at tax filing time.

Funny thing…most Canadians seem quite complacent about this…despite the fact that their non-deductible credit card debt is growing at the same time, and there is no extra money available to pay this or pay down the mortgage, or for an RRSP contribution. Be tax-wise: change this paradigm.

New employment deductions and credits

In recent years, the government has started to recognize that in order to earn that employment income, most employees have out-of-pocket expenses. But, only specific expenses can be deducted under the Income Tax Act; all others are considered to be personal living expenses.

Good news! In July 2006, a $250 *Canada Employment Credit* was introduced to offset employment expenses. For 2008, this amount has increased to $1,019.

The costs of tools by tradespersons and apprentice vehicle mechanics have also been recognized in recent years.

And, if you're a long-haul truck driver, you'll be pleased this year. The deductible claim for meals (discussed later in this chapter) will be increased over the next several years.

Put a tax focus on your employment negotiations

When you know the tax benefits available to you as an employee, you can file a more accurate tax return and negotiate a more lucrative employment contract.

Here's the plan: let's get some extra lift out of your day-to-day efforts at your place of employment. By investing in yourself, your company, and the tax benefits available to employees under the tax system, you'll kick start your own wealth creation.

Essential TAX FACT #23

Employees are restricted in the types of deductions they can claim, but tax advantages can be negotiated for bonuses, salary or wages, sabbaticals, tax free and taxable perks, retirement savings, severance packages and death benefits.

CRA defines an employer-employee relationship as follows:

"A verbal or written agreement in which an employee agrees to work on a full-time or part-time basis for a specified or indeterminate period of time, in return for salary or wages. The employer has the right to decide where, when and how the work will be done. In this type of relationship a contract of service exists."

The employer has several obligations to you to meet in this relationship. An employer is required by law to make statutory deductions from your gross pay for contributions to the Canada Pension Plan (CPP), Employment Insurance (EI) and Income Taxes.

These are usually remitted once a month, although very small businesses have the option to remit each quarter. Minors need not contribute to the Canada Pension Plan; nor do those over 70 (except in Quebec) or those who are in receipt of CPP benefits. Everyone who is employed must contribute to EI; that is, there is no age limit. Employees who earn $2,000 or less from employment will have their premiums refunded when they file their tax returns.

It is also a requirement that the employer prepare a T4 slip for each employee and issue it to the employee by the end of February each year, for use in filing the income tax return. One copy is remitted to CRA at this time as well.

But that T4 slip can contain much more information:

- Commission income against which employment expenses can be claimed
- Deductible union or professional dues
- Deductible contributions to company pension plans
- Creditable charitable donations
- Creditable medical premiums to private health care plans
- Perks that can be offset with tax deductions like the Northern Residents Deductions, auto expenses, carrying charges for low-interest investment loan benefits, Securities Options Deductions, Home Relocation Loan Deductions, RRSP contributions and rollovers, deductions for Worker's Compensation Benefits received.

It's up to you as the employee to claim the correct tax credits and deductions to increase the amount of tax withholding that is returned at the end of the year when the tax return is filed. In fact, you can apply to get the benefit of those increased tax refunds immediately.

You may be familiar with the *TD1 Tax Credit Return*. It's a form you'll complete every time you start a new job, to let your employer know how much income tax to withhold from your pay. It is based on non-refundable tax credits, like your basic personal amount, spousal amount, amount for dependent children, caregiver amounts, tuition and education amounts and the deduction for Northern Residents, and allows you to direct increased tax deductions to cover other income sources you may have during the year.

Essential TAX FACT #24

Proper completion of the *TD1 Personal Tax Credit Return* and its sister, *Form T1213 Request to Reduce Tax Deductions at Source*, will help you pay the right amount of tax all year long.

It will not, however, take into account other tax deductible expenditures you may have all year long like RRSP contributions, deductible spousal support, significant interest costs, rental losses, child care, commission sales or other expenses of employment, medical expenses or large charitable donations. To benefit from these, you need to file *Form T1213*.

This form allows you to ask that less tax be taken from your earnings—a wise move if you want to pay off non-deductible credit card debt or your mortgage, or kick start a more aggressive savings plan. This is the first and best way for you to put more money in your pocket all year long.

Grab these forms off the internet, from your human resource department, or ask your tax or financial advisors to help you.

Diversify employment income

Now that you have taken control of your after-tax employment dollars, it's important to reframe your thinking around your master-servant relationship. You can earn equity as well as employment income, with proper tax planning. There are just a few basics you'll need to know.

Essential TAX FACT #25

Another reason employees overpay their taxes is because they don't diversify their income sources.

There are several sources of employment income within a master-servant relationship:

- Income from salary or wages, which is taxable in the year received
- Director's fees (these are subject to CPP but not EI premiums)

- Employee Benefit Plans like a self-funded leave of absence
- The value of taxable benefits or perks

Employment income is always reported on the cash basis—when received. You will also report your employment income on a calendar year basis— January to December—in every case. Sometimes, an opportunity for salary deferral to a following year may be available.

Under a salary deferral arrangement, receipt of salary or wages is postponed into the future; generally the next tax year. However, here's a trap: the deferred amount is generally included in income in the current year or year of contribution—which means that no tax deferral is actually allowed.

More common and allowable salary deferral can be achieved through a registered plan:

- Registered Pension Plan (RPP)
- Employee Profit Sharing Plan (EPSP)
- Deferred Profit Sharing Plan (DPSP)

In addition, it is possible to defer salary or wages for a self-funded leave or sabbatical. The employee who saves in this way will not be subject to tax in the year the leave is earned as long as salary is deferred for no more than 6 years and no more than $\frac{1}{3}$ of the salary is deferred. The leave of absence must start no later than the 7th year and must be for a period of at least six months. The employee must then return to work for at least the same amount of time as the leave. The amounts are taxable in the year withdrawn.

You should also be aware that there are numerous types of employee benefit plans available. Often the employee will not be taxed when contributions are made to these types of plans but benefits received from them are generally taxable when received. Tax-deferred plans include registered pension plans, group sickness or accident plans, supplementary employment plans, deferred profit sharing plans, wage loss replacement plans, and certain employee trusts.

Therefore, while employment income is usually taxable as received, a few special tax preferences exist to help the employee defer some compensation into the future. Tap into this wherever you can. But start with a good, long term contract and a substantial perk package.

Negotiate the perk package

Taxable benefits are already included in income in Box 14 of the T4 slip so there is no need to add them to income again when you prepare a return. This is a common tax filing error. Taxable benefits include:

- Board and lodging
- Rent-free and low-rent housing
- Travel benefits for the employee and his/her family
- Personal use of an employer-provided vehicle
- The value of holidays, prizes, and other awards
- Frequent flyer program points used for personal use if earned on business trips
- Premiums under provincial hospital plans
- Interest-free or low-interest loans
- The cost of relocation benefits, for example, reimbursement for losses suffered on sale of an old residence, but only one half the amounts over $15,000 must be added to income.

You should also know that certain taxable benefits qualify for deductions on the tax return. These include:

- **Housing, Board and Lodging.** The taxable benefit will include a cleric's housing allowance, rent-free or low-rent apartments provided to caretakers or subsidized meals or travel in a prescribed zone or for medical travel. Board and lodging provided at a remote or special worksite can be received tax free, however. Offsetting deductions may be included for clerics and those who qualify for the northern residents' deduction.

- **Personal Use of Employer's Auto.** An automobile "standby charge" taxable benefit recognizes the personal use

Essential TAX FACT #26

Besides your salary or wage, which is reported on Line 101 of the tax return—from Box 14 of the T4 slip—it is possible to earn taxable or tax free benefits in your employment package.

Essential TAX FACT #27

Employees who use their company car more than 50% for business should discuss the reduction of standby charges with their payroll department.

component of an employer-provided vehicle. It is calculated at 2 per cent per month of the original cost of the vehicle where the employer owns the vehicle, or two-thirds of the lease payment for leased vehicles. However for car sales persons, the benefit is 1½%.

- **Operating Costs.** Amounts paid for the operation of the employer's vehicle will also be taxable as a benefit, unless they are reimbursed by the employee within 45 days after the end of the tax year. The benefit is determined as a flat per kilometre rate, regardless of how or how much the employer paid for the expenses. This rate is announced every year in December. Alternatively, the benefit can be assessed at one half the normal stand-by charge.

- **Reduction in Standby Charges.** It is possible that the employee may offset this benefit with a claim for Employment Expenses using *Form T777 Employment Expenses* or through a reduction in standby charges if personal driving is less than 20,000 kilometers per year and the car is used more than 50% of the time for employment.

- **Interest-Free Loans and Low Interest Loans.** A deduction for the benefit enjoyed from an employer-provided loan will be allowed if you use the loan for investment purposes. This might result, for example, if you borrowed to invest in company shares.

- **Employee Home Relocation Loan Deduction.** A deduction may be possible on Line 248. This is discussed in more detail later.

- **Securities Options Deductions.** A deduction may be possible on Line 249 for those who have generated a taxable benefit from employee stock option purchases and disposals. See details below.

- **Other taxable benefits,** including amounts included in income for health or educational benefits received may qualify for non-refundable credits on the personal tax return—such as medical expenses or tuition, education and textbook amounts.

- **Cost of Tools.** Where your employer makes payments to offset the cost of tools required to perform your work, the amount of the payment must be included in income. However, an offsetting deduction may be allowed for the cost of tools for a tradesperson or an apprentice.

Essential TAX FACT #28

Employment Commissions included in income may be offset by Employment Expenses on Line 229 and the GST Rebate on Line 457 under certain conditions.

Many employees also fail to negotiate for lucrative tax free benefits from their employer. *For a complete list of tax benefits visit www.knowledgebureau.com/ETF.*

- **Employer-Paid Educational Costs.** You are not taxed when training is paid for by your employer for courses taken primarily for the benefit of the employer. However, a taxable benefit arises when the training is primarily for your personal benefit. Amounts included in your income for tuition will be eligible for the tuition tax credit if they would have been eligible had they been paid by you personally.

Essential TAX FACT #29

Employer-paid education costs may be received tax free.

- **Financial Counselling and Income Tax Return Preparation.** Financial counselling services or income tax return preparation provided directly or indirectly by an employer normally produce a taxable benefit. However, financial counselling services in respect of your re-employment or retirement will not result in a taxable benefit.

Essential TAX FACT #30

Other benefits may be taxable, but subject to exceptions that provide for tax free results.

- **Frequent Flyer Points.** CRA takes the position that where you accumulate frequent flyer points while travelling on employer-paid business trips and you use them to obtain air travel or other benefits for personal use by you or your family, the fair market value of such air travel or other benefits must be included in your income. Where an employer does not control the credits accumulated in a frequent flyer program while travelling on employer-paid business trips, it will be your responsibility to determine and include in income the fair market value of any benefits received or enjoyed. This value can be computed as the lowest equivalent ticket price on flights taken for personal use.

Essential TAX FACT #31

Frequent Flyer Points used personally by employees will usually be taxable.

- **Gifts Under $500.** A gift (either in cash or in kind) from your employer is an employment benefit. However, an employer is allowed to give an employee two

Essential TAX FACT #32

An employee can receive up to $500 in non-cash gifts from the employer, tax free.

tax-free, non-cash gifts commemorating a wedding, Christmas or similar occasion or in recognition of service or the reaching of a milestone and still claim those costs as an expense in computing taxable income.

Essential TAX FACT #33

Gifts containing corporate logos may have insignificant tax consequences.

Essential TAX FACT #34

Premiums paid for group term life insurance are considered to be a taxable benefit.

Essential TAX FACT #35

Taxable vacations include use of the employer's vacation property by you, your family or both.

If you are rewarded by your employer with merchandise or other non-cash items, the fair market value of the award must be included in your income. If an item is personalized with a corporate logo or engraved with your name or a message, the fair market value of the item may be negatively affected. In such cases, the amount to be included in income may be reduced by a reasonable amount, having regard to all the circumstances. Depending on the value of a particular award, the existence of a logo may have little, if any, impact on the fair market value of the item. When the award given is a plaque, trophy or other memento of nominal value for which there is no market, it is not necessary to include any amount in your income as a taxable benefit.

- **Vacations.** Where an employer pays for a vacation for you or your family, the cost is considered to be a taxable benefit. In such cases, the benefit is equal to the fair market value of the travel and accommodation less any amount you pay your employer. The taxable benefit may be reduced if there is conclusive evidence to show that you were involved in business activities for your employer during the vacation.

In a situation where your presence is required for business purposes and this function is the main purpose of the trip, no benefit will be associated with the travelling expenses necessary to accomplish the business objectives of the trip if the expenditures are reasonable in relation to the business function.

Where a business trip is extended to provide for a paid holiday or vacation, you are considered to have received a taxable benefit equal to the costs borne by the employer with respect to that extension.

Note that if your spouse accompanies you on a business trip the payment or reimbursement by the employer of the spouse's travelling expenses is a taxable benefit unless the spouse was, in fact, engaged primarily in business activities on behalf of the employer during the trip.

- **Relocation Costs.** If your employer reimburses you for a loss suffered in selling the family home upon being required to move to another locality or upon retirement from employment in a remote area, only a portion of the reimbursement must be included in income as a taxable benefit.

Essential TAX FACT #36

Reimbursement of up to $15,000 of losses on the sale of your home may be tax free, where the employer required the move.

Where the loss and reimbursement are both less than $15,000 no taxable benefit will accrue. Where the loss and reimbursement exceed $15,000 the benefit is one-half of the excess of the reimbursement over $15,000.

Essential TAX FACT #37

The tax status of employer-paid parking has been the subject of court challenges.

- **Employer-Paid Parking.** Parking costs paid by your employer will generally be included as a taxable benefit, calculated at fair market value. Parking is excluded from the value of a stand-by charge, or auto operating expense benefits, or benefits for disabled employees. However, recent court challenges have found in favour of the taxpayer in establishing a non-taxable status for parking, when it was found to be in the employer's favour to offer parking to employees.

Ensure peace of mind on health care

The tax status of premiums paid and benefits received from employer-sponsored group and non-group health plans can be confusing, but is very important in the overall scheme of compensation to the employee. These plans can provide important peace of mind when expensive health care costs arise.

Essential TAX FACT #38

Premiums paid by the employer under provincial hospitalization and medical care insurance plans are taxable; private plans are not.

Essential TAX FACT #39

Many provincial prescription plans require information from the personal tax return to determine deductible levels. Be sure to file these forms when you do your taxes every year.

Taxable Status of Premiums Paid. Premiums will be taxable in two instances: where the employer pays or reimburses you for the employee portion of premiums to a provincial health care plan; or where the employer pays some or all of the premium under a non-group plan that is a wage loss replacement, sickness or accident insurance plan, a disability insurance plan, or an income maintenance insurance plan. However, payroll source deductions made for the payment of the premiums are considered to be payments made by you, not the employer.

If the wage loss replacement plan is a group plan, or if the health care plan is private, then the employer's portion of the premiums paid is not considered to be a taxable benefit.

Taxable Status of Wage Loss Replacement Benefits Received. If you paid all of the premiums to a wage loss replacement plan, then periodic payments (or a lump sum paid in lieu of periodic payments) from the plan are tax-free and should not be reported on an information slip.

If the plan was funded, in whole or in part, by the employer, then the benefits received are taxable, but you are entitled to a deduction for the lesser of the amount received from the plan and all premiums that you have paid since 1968 and not previously deducted. The deduction should be claimed on Line 229 of the tax return.

Maximize tax-assisted retirement savings options

An employer may assist in maximizing retirement savings using the tax department as an active participant in wealth accumulation. There are numerous ways to do so.

Begin by adjusting source deductions for income taxes on each payroll period to take into account the deductible portion of employee contributions to Registered Pension Plans (RPPs) and Registered Retirement Savings Plans

(RRSPs). Then know the details of tax deferred accumulation, severance rollovers and withdrawal. Here are some basic rules:

Registered Pension Plans. A registered pension plan (RPP) is a private pension plan set up for employees, which has been registered with the Minister of National Revenue. The plan may be instituted by the employer or a trade union in cooperation with the employer. The employer must make contributions to the plan. The plan may be structured as a defined benefit or a money purchase arrangement or a combination of the two. It is important as you negotiate a new employment contract to find out the details.

Under a *money purchase* plan the employer and employee contributions in each member's separate account accumulate investment earnings on a tax-deferred basis and the sum total determines the size of pension benefits that can be purchased at retirement. There is no promise that a certain level of retirement benefits will be provided and no uncertainty regarding the employer's financial obligation to the plan.

A *defined benefit* plan on the other hand, is a plan under which the ultimate retirement benefits promised are determined by formula. The employee's contributions are predetermined and the employer generally contributes whatever is required to ensure those promised retirement benefits materialize.

An employee may make contributions to an RPP:

- for the current year or
- for past service for years after 1990.

Current year employee contributions. These amounts are tax deductible and appear in Box 20 of your T4 slip or on a union dues receipt. They are only deductible in the current tax year and may not be carried over to another taxation year.

Past service contributions for service before 1990. In addition, you may deduct, within limits, your contributions to an RPP in respect of service in years before 1990. Such amounts are included in Box 20, 74 and 75 of your T4 slip. The deduction limitations are complicated, as shown below:

- *Employee contributions for pre-1990 past service while not a contributor* – You may deduct the least of:

Essential TAX FACT #40

Any past service contributions that are not deductible may be carried forward to a subsequent year and deducted with the same limitations.

– contributions made in the year or a previous year in respect of such service less deductions previously claimed
– $3,500
– $3,500 per year of such service to which you made past service contributions minus deductions previously claimed in respect of those contributions and deductions claimed before 1987 for "additional voluntary contributions"

- *Employee contributions for pre-1990 past service while a contributor* – Deduct the lesser of:
  – The amount of the contributions made in the year, or a previous year, less deductions previously claimed
  – $3,500 minus the amount deducted in the year for
    ~ current service
    ~ post-1989 past service contributions and
    ~ pre-1990 past service contributions while not a contributor

Any amounts contributed but not deductible may be carried forward to a subsequent year and deducted with the same limitations.

Your ability to claim undeducted past service contributions carried forward is not affected by changes in employment status. That is, you may retire or change companies and still be allowed to deduct past service pension plan contributions carried forward.

Pension Adjustments. This is a term you need to know. Employees who are members of a Registered Pension Plan will be assigned a Pension Adjustment for the year. This is reported in Box 52 of the T4 slip or Box 34 of the T4A slip and decreases your RRSP contribution limit for the year. You should also know that employees who contribute in

Essential
TAX FACT #41

When a taxpayer dies, the deduction of unclaimed past service contributions in the year of death may be made in full, without regard to the $3,500 per year limitations.

Essential
TAX FACT #42

It is generally not possible to claim the cost of interest on money borrowed to contribute to a registered pension plan as a carrying charge.

Essential
TAX FACT #43

Pension adjustments are not considered to be income but limit the deduction available for RRSP contributions.

respect of past service will also be assigned a "Past Service Pension Adjustment" (PSPA).

Note that benefits received from a registered pension plan are taxable. In some cases, they may qualify for the Pension Income credit.

See Part Five for more details on the Registered Retirement Savings Plan (RRSP) and its contribution limits—an important cornerstone of retirement savings you will want to tap into to supplement your superannuation in retirement.

Leverage using the employer's capital pool

Employees should always strive to build capital—assets that can produce other sources of income or grow in value. One way to do so is to use your employer's money—at preferred low or no-interest rates. This however, will give rise to a taxable benefit.

For example, the employer may loan funds to you or your spouse. In either case, a taxable benefit would accrue to you, unless your spouse is also an employee of the same employer. The same rules will apply when you receive a loan from a third party, if the employer is involved in securing the loan for you.

On a no-interest loan, the amount of the benefit is equal to:

- the interest on the loan at CRA's currently prescribed rate (see Part One for details for the current tax year), plus
- any payments made by the employer, less
- amounts of interest paid back by you to the employer either during the year or within 30 days after the end of the year.

This benefit is included in your income and will be reported on your T4.

If the loan bears interest, there is no taxable benefit where the interest rate on the loan is

Essential TAX FACT #44

If the employer-provided loan was used to acquire income-producing investments, the amount of the interest benefit shown on the T4 will be deductible as a carrying charge.

Essential TAX FACT #45

It is important to determine if the loan was granted because the taxpayer was an employee or a shareholder of the company.

equal to or greater than a commercial rate so long as you actually pay the interest. Special rules apply to housing loans and home relocation loans, discussed later.

Note: These rules apply to shareholders as well as to employees. The difference between a shareholder loan and an employee loan is that the benefit accrues to the employee, even if the loan is to someone else. However, the benefit accrues to the debtor if the loan is a shareholder loan.

This is because of a special anti-avoidance rule that prevents a shareholder from indefinitely postponing the recognition of income from a corporation by taking continuous shareholder loans. Professional help should be sought to report these transactions.

Where the shareholder is also an employee, certain loans will be allowed the treatment given to any employee if it can be established that bona fide loan arrangements are made, the loan is repaid over a reasonable period of time and the loan is a direct result of the employer-employee relationship. This means that the company must make similar loans available to all employees.

Tap into equity with employee stock option plans

Employees may be presented with an opportunity to purchase shares in the employer's corporation at some future date, but at a price set at the time the option was granted. This is known as the exercise price.

When you exercise these stock or security options a taxable benefit arises, equal to the difference between the market value of the shares purchased and the exercise price.

When is this taxable? It depends on the type of corporation.

If the employer is a Canadian Controlled Private Corporation (CCPC), the taxable benefit is deemed to arise when you dispose of the shares.

In the case of a public corporation, the taxable benefit arises when you exercise the option. However, you can elect to defer the benefit to a future year.

Note this important date: You must express your intention to defer the security option benefits to your employer by January 16 of the year after the year in which the option is exercised, so that the deferred amount may be included on your T4 slip.

The taxable benefit may not be deferred:

- if you emigrate from Canada or
- in the year of death.

It is wise to get some professional help before stock options are acquired or disposed of, as certain technical provisions must be observed. If the shares acquired under such a stock option are donated to a registered charity or to a private foundation (after March 19, 2007), you may claim a deduction equal to the taxable benefit.

Essential TAX FACT #48

There are no tax consequences when an employee stock option is granted.

Essential TAX FACT #49

When the security options taxable benefit is included in income, you may also be eligible for the Security Options Deduction which is equal to one-half of the taxable benefit.

Maximize employment deductions

The *Income Tax Act* is very specific about the expenses that may be claimed by employees. However, you can claim a credit designed to offset your employment expenses. This credit, claimed on line 363 of Schedule 1 is based on $1,019 for 2008 (assuming you earned at least that much employment income in the year). For most employees, this is the only tax relief for employment expenses. Employment deductions are generally claimed on *Form T777 Employment Expenses* and require the completion and signing of *Form T2200 Declaration of Conditions of Employment* by the employer.

Essential TAX FACT #50

Employees are entitled to the Canada Employment Credit to help offset their employment expenses.

Special, more generous deductions are allowed to the commissioned sales employee. Those who are not commissioned may deduct the following out-of-pocket expenses, but only up to the amount of their earnings from employment; no carry over of deductions is allowed to the following year with the exception of home workspace expenses.

Visit www.knowledgebureau.com/ETF for Essential Tax Fact Sheets on the details of employment expenses and special rules for artists and musicians.

Essential
TAX FACT #51

Tradespersons may claim a deduction for the cost of new tools purchased for use in their job if they spend over $1,019 in a year.

Essential
TAX FACT #52

Long distance truckers and other employees in the transport business may deduct certain unreimbursed board and lodging expenses.

Special deductions for tradespeople. A tradesperson who is required to purchase new tools for use in employment may deduct the cost in excess of $1,019 (to a maximum of $500 for 2008). This claim, which is made on line 229 of the tax return, will only be accepted if the employer certifies (on *Form T2200*) that you are required to purchase your own tools for use in your job as a tradesperson. This deduction is in addition to the Canada Employment Credit.

Special Rules for Transport Employees. If an employee of an airline, rail company, trucking company or other such organization whose main business is the transport of goods or passengers must:

- regularly travels away from the municipality or metropolitan area where the home terminal is located, and

- use vehicles provided by the employer to transport goods or passengers

a deduction may be claimed for meals and lodging while on the road.

It is possible to claim the cost of meals using one of two methods:

- the "simplified method": here unreceipted claims can be made for one meal every four hours from check-out time, up to a maximum of three meals per 24-hour period at a flat rate per meal. Currently, and since 2006, this is $17.00 per meal (maximum $51.00 per 24 hour period). For trips in the US, the amount is $17.00 US. The rate from 2003 to 2005 was $15.00 and from 1990 to 2002 was $11.00 per meal.

- the "detailed method," whereby claims are made according to actual receipts submitted.

Note: When a transport employee who is normally required to travel out of town is on a scheduled run of ten hours or less they are expected to eat before and after work and therefore may only claim one meal per day. Special rules also apply for crews of workers who are provided cooking facilities. Under the "batching method", receipts are not required but the claim is limited to the equivalent of two meals per day (currently $34.00).

If you claim deductible expenses, including the *Claim for Board and Lodging* (which requires completion of *Form TL2* and signature by the employer) you may receive a rebate of the GST/HST paid, discussed later. Rebates are added to income in the year received. You must support the claims with time and distance logs.

Special Rules for Long-Haul Drivers. In the March 2007 federal budget the finance department announced a plan to increase the deduction for meals available to certain long-haul truck drivers. The plan is to increase the percentage of the claim that can be made, starting with an increase to 60% for meals purchased after March 18, 2007. The rate will be increased by 5% each year until it reaches 80% in 2011. For 2008, the percentage claimable is 65%. Like all other transport employees, the claim for meals purchased before March 19, 2007 is 50% of the expense amount.

The enhanced deduction is limited to an employee whose principal duty or an individual whose principal business is to drive a long-haul truck in transporting goods, and to employers who pay or reimburse such expenses. To qualify for the enhanced deduction:

- the long-haul truck must have a gross vehicle weight rating in excess of 11,788 kg,

- the driver must be away for at least 24 continuous hours from the employer's municipality or metropolitan area to which the employee reports (employed drivers) or the municipality where the driver resides (self-employed drivers);

- the trip must involve the transport of goods to or from a location at least 160 km from the location described above.

Special Rules for Northern Residents. Individuals who resided in a pre-scribed northern or intermediate zone for a period of at least six consecutive months beginning or ending in a taxation year will qualify to claim a Northern Residents Deduction, and in some cases, a deduction for travel benefits provided by the employer or a member of the employee's household for travel expenses incurred in connection with any trips made to obtain medical services not available locally and up to two trips per year for other reasons, to the extent that the value of these benefits is included in employment income. For 2008, both the basic residency amount and the additional residency amounts available increased from $7.50 per day to $8.25 per day. Form T2222 Northern Residents Deductions must be filed with the return.

Make special claims for commission salespeople

If you earn your living negotiating contracts for your employer or selling on commission you may claim expenses for travel and sales costs under these circumstances:

- you are required to pay your own expenses
- you regularly perform your duties away from the employer's place of business
- you do not receive a tax-free travel allowance.

Deductible travel expenses allowed include:

- automobile-related operating expenses like gas, oil, repairs and fixed costs like licenses, insurance, interest, leasing and Capital Cost Allowance. The latter three expenses are limited to certain annual maximums if a passenger or luxury vehicle is used. This is discussed in more detail later.
- the cost of air, bus, rail, taxi or other transportation which takes the employee outside the employer's metropolitan area.

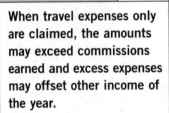

Essential TAX FACT #54

When travel expenses only are claimed, the amounts may exceed commissions earned and excess expenses may offset other income of the year.

Essential TAX FACT #55

Sales expenses may exceed commissions earned in the calendar year except for interest and capital cost allowance on a motor vehicle.

Deductible sales expenses allowed include promotional expenses, entertainment expenses (subject to the 50% restriction), travel, auto and home office costs.

Note: Employees are not allowed to make a claim for capital expenditures with the exception of the purchase of vehicles, musical instruments or aircraft and a tradesperson's tools. Therefore it is more tax efficient to lease computers, cell phones or other equipment, or ask the employer to pay for these.

Audit-proof auto allowances and expenses

Auto Allowances. When you receive an additional amount as an auto allowance from your employer, in addition to salary or wages, the amounts will generally be taxable, unless the amount is "reasonable".

Reasonable tax free travel allowances include:

- Travel allowances paid to members of the Canadian Forces,

- Reasonable allowances for travel expenses paid to a commission salesman,

- Reasonable allowances for travel expenses paid to a clergyman,

- Reasonable allowances for use of a motor vehicle paid to an employee for travel in the performance of the employee's duties,

- Reasonable allowances received by Members of Parliament.

An allowance is deemed not to be reasonable unless it is based solely on business related kilometers driven. It is also deemed not to be reasonable, and is therefore taxable, if you are also reimbursed for actual expenditures (exception: your employer may reimburse for supplementary insurance charges, toll or ferry charges). Amounts paid to part-time employees (such as visiting professors) may also qualify under these rules, as long as:

Essential TAX FACT #56

To be considered reasonable, the allowances must be based solely on the number of kilometres driven.

- the employer and employee are dealing at arm's length

- the employee had other employment or was self-employed and

- the duties of employment were performed more than 80 kilometres from the employee's residence and other employment/self-employment.

Reasonable amounts paid in advance (on a periodic basis) by your employer may also be excluded from income if:

- they are based on distance travelled (i.e. a cents per kilometre basis),
- the rate is reasonable,
- you are required to report distance travelled for business purposes, and
- there is a year-end reconciliation of distance travelled to amounts advanced and you are required to repay any excess amounts received.

A prescribed per kilometre rate is generally stated by CRA each year as the reasonable rate to use in calculating these amounts.

Where the allowance is not reasonable the whole amount of the allowance is included in computing your income and, if you qualify, an appropriate amount may be deducted for actual travel expenses.

Special rules also exist for those employed at a remote worksite.

Auto Expenses. Auto expenses are one of the most common deductions for the employed and self-employed and also amongst the most audited. Therefore it is important to understand the rules surrounding "mixed use".

Personal use includes vehicle use by other family members, friends, etc. and travel to and from the place of business or employment.

To make the claim on a tax return, actual expenses are first totalled, using the actual receipts and/or log of cash expenditures like car washes or parking meters. Then the total amount expended and so supported is pro-rated by the portion of business/employment kilometres over the total kilometres driven in the year.

Starting in 2009, a logbook maintained to track employment/personal driving for "a sample period of time" instead of a calendar full year will suffice for tax audit purposes.

Essential TAX FACT #57

An allowance will be considered unreasonable (and therefore taxable) if you are paid a combined flat rate and per-kilometer rate allowance.

Essential TAX FACT #58

If you use your vehicle for both personal and business/employment purposes, it is necessary to keep an auto log that records distance driven for each purpose.

Automotive expenses can only be deducted if they are not reimbursed by your employer or business. If they are reimbursed, but the amount of the reimbursement is not reasonable, the reimbursement can be shown as income and the actual auto expenses otherwise deductible (as discussed above) can be deducted in computing net income.

Essential TAX FACT #59

Only parking costs can be claimed in full. No "cents-per-kilometer" claims are allowed.

To claim auto expenses, you must pay your own auto expenses and be required to use your vehicle in carrying out duties of employment. *Form T2200* must be signed by your employer. You cannot claim auto expenses if you are in receipt of a non-taxable reasonable allowance from your employer.

Essential TAX FACT #60

There are two types of auto expenses that can be claimed: fixed expenses and operating costs.

Operating costs include gas, oil, maintenance, repairs, insurance and auto club memberships. However other "fixed" expenses are subject to restrictions; specifically these are Capital Cost Allowance or CCA, leasing and interest costs. These limitations apply where you acquire a vehicle with a capital cost of more than $30,000 plus taxes or for which a lease of more than $800 plus taxes is paid per month. Also restricted are interest costs—a maximum of $300 a month or $10 per day is allowed under current rules.

If you own your own vehicle, or purchase one, you cannot deduct the whole cost of the vehicle in one year, but you are allowed to claim a portion of the cost each year under the Capital Cost Allowance (CCA) system. Under this system, you can deduct a specified percentage of the undepreciated capital cost (UCC) of the asset each year. The UCC is the cost of the vehicle less the CCA claims you made in prior years. For the purposes of claiming Capital Cost Allowance, expensive vehicles are scheduled in Class 10.1, and each vehicle has its own class. Only $30,000 (plus taxes) of the cost is added to the CCA pool. Other vehicles (including those known as motor vehicles and autos which are not passenger vehicles) are placed in Class 10, which features a "pooling" of capital costs.

In each Class 10 and Class 10.1, the undepreciated capital cost qualifies for a 30% CCA rate, and all other deductibility rules are similar, including a special half-year rule on acquisition. However, in addition to the restriction on the capital cost itself, there are several differences in tax results when the asset is disposed of. What you need to know, before you buy or lease a vehicle, is this that passenger or luxury vehicles will result in a restricted claim for CCA, interest or leasing costs and this tax result should be taken into account.

Visit www.knowledgebureau.com/ETF for more information on keeping auto logs.

Write off the home office

Many employees and self-employed work out of their home and may make legitimate claims for the cost of running a home workspace. What is important is to prorate total costs to remove any personal use component by the following fraction:

$$\frac{\text{Square footage of the home workspace}}{\text{Square footage of the entire living area}} \quad \text{X} \quad \frac{\text{Total Eligible}}{\text{Expenses}} \quad = \quad \frac{\text{Deductible}}{\text{Expenses}}$$

Claims by Employees. You may not claim home office expenses in excess of income from employment for the tax year.

Essential TAX FACT #61

Non-deductible home office expenses may be carried forward and are treated as having been incurred in the next year.

In order to claim home office expenses you must have a *Form T2200* signed by your employer to certify that you are required to maintain the home office and pay the expenses of operating it. Your claims for home office expenses are made on *Form T777 Statement of Employment Expenses*.

See www.knowledgebureau.com/ETF for a list of Deductible Home Workspace Expenses.

Tap into often-missed GST rebates

Employees who claim employment expenses on Line 229 or union and professional dues on Line 212 and who are not in receipt of a reasonable auto allowance for those expenses may apply for a cash rebate of any GST or HST paid on these expenses on Line 457 of the tax return. *Form GST 370* must be completed.

Expenses eligible for the rebate include:

- office expenses
- travel expenses
- entertainment expenses
- meals and lodging (deductible portion only)
- motor vehicle expenses
- leasing costs
- parking cost
- miscellaneous supplies (e.g. street maps, stamps, pens, pencils, and paper clips), and
- capital cost allowance on motor vehicles, aircraft, and musical instruments acquired after 1990.

In the case of GST, with the reduction in the GST rate to 5% on January 1, 2008, the rebate is 5/105 of the expenses on which GST was paid. In the case of HST, the rebate is 13/113 of the expenses.

Essential TAX FACT #62

Members of a partnership that is a GST/HST registrant may also claim this rebate on the expenses that are deductible from their share of the partnership income.

Essential TAX FACT #63

Taxpayers who have failed to claim the *GST/HST Rebate* in prior years may file adjustments to recover this credit for the prior 10 year period.

In the year the GST/HST rebate is received, the portion that relates to current expenses must be reported as income on Line 104. The portion that relates to a capital asset (vehicle, musical instrument or airplane) must be used to reduce the UCC of the class to which the asset belongs.

Claim lucrative moving expenses

Lucrative moving deductions can be claimed on Line 219 using *Form T1-M*. To qualify, the taxpayer must earn salary, wages, or self-employment income at the new location. In addition, the taxpayer must stop working or operating a business at the old location, and establish a new home where the taxpayer and family will reside. Students who move to attend post-secondary education may claim moving expenses against the taxable amount of scholarships and bursaries.

The following income sources earned at the new location will not be considered "qualifying income" for the purposes of claiming moving expenses:

- investment income

Essential TAX FACT #64

To be eligible, the new home must be at least 40 km closer to the new work location than the old home.

Essential TAX FACT #65

Travel expenses may be calculated using a rate per kilometre basis rather than claiming the actual amount spent. Meals can be claimed on a flat rate, too.

Essential TAX FACT #66

If income at the new location does not sufficiently offset all moving expenses in the year of the move, expenses may be carried forward and applied against income at the new location in the following year.

- employment insurance benefits
- other income sources, except student awards (see below).

The distance of the move is measured by the shortest normal route open to the travelling public. Generally the move must be within Canada although students may claim moving expenses to attend a school outside Canada if they are otherwise eligible.

Expenses for moves between two locations outside Canada may be possible if you are a deemed resident or factual resident of Canada and the move was from the place you ordinarily resided, to a new place where you will ordinarily reside.

Visit www.knowledgebureau.com/ETF for a list of deductible and non-deductible moving expenses.

The simplified method (see Tax Fact #65) does not require receipts to be kept for travel expenses, only a record of the distance traveled during the move. The rate is calculated based on the province in which the move began. Meals en route may also be charged at a flat rate per meal ($17.00 at the time of writing) with a maximum of three meals per day (total $51.00) per family member. For ongoing current rates, visit the CRA web site at http://www.ccra-adrc.gc.ca/travelcosts.

Note: If you receive reimbursements for moving expenses you may only deduct expenses if the amount received as a reimbursement is included in income, or if the amounts claimed are reduced by the amount of the reimbursement.

Employee Home Relocation Deduction. When an employer relocates an employee to another area, the employer may offer the employee a low-interest or no-interest loan to assist with the costs of relocating. The difference between the interest charged on the loan and the interest calculated at the prescribed interest rate is a taxable benefit and included on the employee's T4 Slip. If you receive this benefit you may qualify for the Employee Home Relocation Loan Deduction claimed on Line 248.

Essential TAX FACT #67

The home relocation loan deduction is available for the first five years of the loan, and, if the loan is $25,000 or less, is equal to the taxable benefit charged the employee.

If the term for repayment for the home relocation loan is more than five years, the balance owing at the end of five years (from the day the loan was made) is considered a new loan. The taxable benefit will be calculated as if the loan were made at that time. However, in this case, no home relocation loan deduction is available.

The rules for the calculation of benefits for a home relocation loan are similar as for any employer-provided loan. The difference is that for a home purchase loan and a home relocation loan the prescribed interest rate used for the calculation of the taxable benefit is the rate in effect at the time the loan is made.

Plan for tax wise terminations

All good things may one day come to and end. When it comes to the end of the road with your employer, consider these tax consequences of termination:

- **Plan a Tax-Free Rollover of Your Termination or Severance into an RRSP.** The amount eligible for rollover to your (but not your spouse's) RRSP depends on when service was provided to the employer:
  - For service after 1995, *no amount* of severance can be rolled over to an RRSP and therefore the full amount is exposed to income taxes.
  - For service *after 1988 and before 1996*, a single limit of $2,000 per year of service can be rolled over.
  - For service *before 1989*, it is possible to roll over $2,000 for each year of service plus $1,500 for each year in which none of your employer's contributions to a company pension plan vested in you.

  Remember, if you can't rollover any amounts by virtue of employment after 1996, top up unused RRSP contribution room and take this deduction against the exposed income. Then, plan to make any taxable withdrawals from the RRSP as required while you hunt for new work. If the withdrawal occurs in a year in which income falls into a lower tax bracket, you'll see a net tax saving from this strategy.

Also, the possibility of taking severance over two taxation years should be explored to determine whether the tax brackets and rates at which the income will be taxed can be reduced, and whether eligibility for social benefits, like the Child Tax Benefit, can be created.

- **EI Maximization.** Employment Insurance benefits you may receive throughout the year will be clawed back when you file your income tax return, if your net income for the tax year is $51,375 or higher and you've received EI benefits in the prior ten years. This can be avoided with astutely planned RRSP contributions.

- **CTB Creation.** Many high income earners who find themselves unemployed often fail to plan for new eligibility for Child Tax Benefits, because they didn't qualify for them in the past. These refundable monthly payments are maximized at family net income levels just under $38,000, but partial benefits may be paid if income is above this, depending on the number of children in the home.

- **Medical Expense Deductibility.** Taxpayers often forget that group health benefits end with employment. Negotiate for continuation wherever possible.

CHAPTER REFLECTION: ESSENTIAL TAX FACTS FOR EMPLOYEES

1. Employees are restricted in the types of deductions they can claim, but tax advantages can be negotiated for:
   - bonuses, salary or wages,
   - sabbaticals,
   - tax free and taxable perks,
   - retirement savings,
   - severage packages and death benefits.

2. Proper completion of the *TD1 Personal Tax Credit Return* and its sister, *Form T1213 Request to Reduce Tax Deductions at Source,* will help you pay the right amount of tax all year long.

3. Another reason employees overpay their taxes is because they don't diversity their income sources.

4. Employees should discuss the reduction of automobile standby charges with their payroll department.

5. Employees should also check out several tax free benefits:
   - The value of apprentice mechanic's tools paid by the employer,
   - Employer-paid education costs,
   - Financial counselling for re-employment or retirement,
   - Up to $500 in non-cash gifts,
   - Gifts containing corporate logos,
   - Reimbursement of up to $15,000 of losses on the sale of your home, if the employer required the move, plus one half of any excess up to the amount of the loss,
   - Premiums paid for private health insurance premiums.

6. Several opportunities exist to buy back and claim deductions for past contributions under Registered Pension Plans.

7. Note that pension adjustments resulting from contributions to Registered Pension Plans at work will limit the deduction available to the taxpayer for RRSP purposes.

8. When an employer-provided loan is used to acquire income-producing investments, the amount of the interest benefit shown on the T4 will be deductible as a carrying charge.

9. When an employer-provided loan is forgiven, however, or settled for an amount less than the principal outstanding, the forgiven amount must be included in your income.

10. Employee stock options offer an excellent way to tap into equity and earn tax-deferred capital.

11. Commissioned salespeople and long distance truckers may each claim meal expenses, but they will be subject to restrictions.

12. Employees may claim the Canada Employment Credit.

13. A tradesperson who is required to purchase tools for use in their employment as a tradesperson may claim a portion of the cost of tools purchased.

14. Auto expenses and allowances have a variety of tax consequences and must be supported by an auto log to be deductible.

15. Taxpayers who acquire luxury or "passenger vehicles" will be subject to restrictions on their capital cost, leasing and interest expenses.

16. Home office expenses may be deductible, however, they may not be used to create a loss from employment or business. Excess expenses may be carried forward, though, to offset future income.

17. The GST rebate is often missed by those who claim professional or union dues on Line 212 of the tax return or employment expenses on Line 229. If so, adjust tax returns for the previous 10 year period.

18. Lucrative moving expenses may be claimed by those who transfer to new work locations.

19. Be sure to plan for tax-wise terminations—tax on severance packages can often be minimized.

20. In tough times, avoid paying a clawback of Employment Insurance benefits (this may happen when net income exceeds $51,375) if you can use an RRSP contribution to reduce income. Seasonal high income construction workers or executives who receive a pink slip late in the year are especially susceptible to this situation.

KEEP CURRENT—WHAT'S NEW?

- All employees are eligible to claim the Canada Employment Credit, starting in 2006. For 2008 the credit amount increased to $1,019.

- If you are a tradesperson and must purchase tools for use in your employment as a tradesperson, you may claim a portion of the amount spent.

- Long-haul truck drivers claims for meals purchased after March 18, 2007 are increased. In 2008, 65% of the outlay for food or beverage expenses is eligible for the claim.

- Canada Pension Plan and Employment Insurance Benefit rates change annually. See *Essential Tax Fact Sheets* for new rates.

NOW PUT MORE MONEY IN YOUR POCKET ALL YEAR LONG...

PERSPECTIVE

We started this chapter by telling you the average tax refund hovers around the $1,440 a year mark or about $120 a month. When you choose to invest that money into a tax-assisted plan like an RRSP instead you'll not only accumulate $1,440 in capital, but you'll save on your taxes too—just under $500 if your taxable income is around $35,000... just over $600 if your income is around $75,000, depending on where you live.

A 33% to 43% after-tax return on your investment is not bad these days.

Never overpay your taxes...*pay yourself first*. Use another method of forced savings. Instruct your employer to deposit $50 per pay cheque into your RRSP account. Make this happen by:

- Reducing your withholding taxes immediately. Fill out the *TD1 Tax Credit Return* your employer gives you at the start of each year properly. Don't fall into that trap of "claiming single" on your TD1!

- Completing *Form T1213 Request to Reduce Tax Deductions at Source*, if you're going to make a direct deposit to your RRSP through your payroll—or if you will have significant charitable donations, child care expenses, tax deductible alimony payments, deductible employment expenses, interest or carrying charges on investment loans, or proprietorship or rental property losses.

- Investing your refund following sound money management rules. Think about your RRSP as your first investment. Then use those tax savings to
  - Eliminate non-deductible debt (like credit cards) with your tax refund,
  - Pay down your non-deductible mortgage interest,
  - Open a non-registered savings account to start accumulating a diverse income stream from interest, dividends, real estate investments or capital gains.

We'll show you how in the next several chapters...

EMPLOYEES

PART FOUR

ESSENTIAL TAX FACTS
FOR SINGLES AND SENIORS

What's important?

Consider the following statistics from the last Canadian census (2006):

- One in seven Canadians, or more than four million, are now elderly.
- The proportion of very elderly—aged 80 and over—increased by 25 per cent between 2001 and 2006, second only to the rate of growth of those aged 55 to 64, and surpassed the one-million mark.
- Two thirds of the very elderly were women.

Even if you are living in a conjugal relationship today, the chances that you may become single again are high from the circumstances of death or divorce or the choice of single parenthood. Often singles are taxed at higher overall rates because it is not possible to split or transfer income and deductions.

However, several notable and new provisions do exist. In this part we will help you answer several key questions by providing Essential Tax Facts for those singles and seniors:

1. What deductions can be claimed by single taxpayers?
2. What refundable tax credit is specifically designed to assist low income earners to come back into the workforce?
3. How do claims for dependants differ for single parents?
4. Can single taxpayers split income with other taxpayers?

5. Young singles often work as waiters or waitresses. What special tax traps must they avoid?

6. Are the cost of mechanics tools deductible?

7. Is mortgage interest paid tax deductible?

8. What should you do: pay down the mortgage or invest in an RRSP?

9. Can you claim anything on the return for supporting a non-resident spouse?

10. What is the difference between the Amount for Minor Children and the Child Tax Benefit?

11. How long must you live apart from your common-law partner to be considered single?

12. Can you claim legal fees paid to get a divorce?

13. What can you claim for caring for an infirm parent who lives with you?

14. What medical expenses can be claimed for dependent adults?

15. What is the real value of making a $500 donation?

What's new?

Check out changes outlined in Part One and this chapter for details about the following:

- Singles who live with dependants for the first time this year may qualify for increased personal amounts
- Seniors will want to check out new clawback zones for the age amount and Old Age Security
- Planning for private retirement savings and pension income splitting continue to benefit Canadian taxpayers.
- The New Registered Disability Savings Plan (RDSP) can help build wealth for the disabled.
- The New Tax-Free Savings Account (TFSA) can assist singles and families build tax exempt savings.
- New medical expenses which can be claimed for you and your dependants.
- New qualifying investments can be donated tax free to charity.

Tax preferences for single taxpayers

Tax and the single taxpayer...the best way to look at this phenomenon is along life's highway. The young and single need to focus on tax advantages unique to their age group:

- Your first post-secondary degree or diploma
- Your first job
- Your retirement savings
- Your first home
- Your first conjugal relationship
- Your mobility—tax deductible moving

After life's firsts, come life's transitions: to every thing, there is a season:

- Separation or divorce
- Single parenthood
- Your second and subsequent post-secondary degrees or diplomas
- Caregiving for adult family members
- Death and taxes

Before delving into the tax specifics of some of the issues above, you'll need to know the following: if you are single, affluent and don't have dependants, you will often bear the full burden of progressivity within our tax system— that is, the more income you realize, the higher your tax bracket and tax rate and the more you will pay—usually with the benefit of only one personal tax credit, instead of several within a family household. You may, however, qualify to take advantage of certain tax preferences: deductions, income-tested tax credits and social benefits, depending on your personal circumstances, as summarized below.

Tax preferences available to singles, with no dependants

Deductions:
- Registered Pension Plan and RRSP contributions
- Union or professional dues
- Disability supports deduction
- Business investment losses
- Moving expenses

- Support payments
- Carrying charges
- Other deductions on lines 222 to 256 of the tax return

Refundable tax credits:
- Federal GST credit
- Working Income Tax Benefit
- Provincial refundable tax credits
- Refundable medical expense supplement
- Refundable investment tax credits
- Employee and partner GST/HST rebate

Non-refundable tax credits:
- The basic personal amount
- The age amount if you have attained age 65
- CPP and EI contributions
- Canada Employment Credit
- Transit pass amount
- Pension income amount (if you are receiving qualifying superannuation)
- Disability amount
- Amount for interest paid on student loans
- Tuition, education and textbook amounts
- Medical expenses
- Donations and gifts

When you add dependants to the mix, singles may also qualify for the following tax preferences:

Deductions:
- Child care expenses

Refundable tax credits:
- Federal and provincial Child Tax Benefits
- Working Income Tax Benefit
- Enhanced GST Credits
- Enhanced provincial credits

Non-refundable tax credits:
- Amount for eligible dependant (formerly known as equivalent-spouse amount)
- Amount for dependent children under 18
- Amount for children's fitness

- Amount for infirm dependants age 18 or older
- Caregiver amount
- Adoption Expense Credit
- Disability amount transferred from dependant
- Tuition, education and textbook amounts transferred from a child
- Medical expenses for other dependants
- Transit pass credit incurred by dependants

The actual dollar amounts assigned to these provisions can change every year, due to indexing or the introduction of new measures in government budgets. Check out recent figures in *Essential Tax Fact Sheets* available at www.knowledgebureau.com/ETF, and discuss current changes with your tax advisor.

What happens when others want to split income with singles? First, know that all the normal Attribution Rules discussed in prior chapters will apply to transfers between related parties.

Singles must also be mindful of the Attribution Rules surrounding their gifts to minors. For example, Sonia, a single 40 year old, wants to give her 10-year-old niece, Jamie, a $10,000 cash gift for investment purposes. Resulting interest, dividends, or royalties are taxed in Sonia's hands. However, resulting capital gains are taxed in Jamie's hands.

Elizabeth, a 48-year-old widow, on the other hand, wants to gift her 10 year old nephew, Vincent, who lives in Europe, a $10,000 lump sum for investment purposes. In that case, there are no Attribution Rules, as Vincent lives abroad.

When it comes to their investments, singles need to look after "No. 1"—you need to minimize the tax you pay on current earnings, and learn discipline in savings strategies even if you are mobile. You can own one tax exempt principal residence, and that's a good place to starting investing.

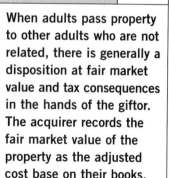

Essential TAX FACT #68

Singles who live alone will be unable to split income with other dependants in the traditional sense, but they may give gifts to those within their family circle. When that happens the Attribution Rules may apply.

Essential TAX FACT #69

When adults pass property to other adults who are not related, there is generally a disposition at fair market value and tax consequences in the hands of the giftor. The acquirer records the fair market value of the property as the adjusted cost base on their books.

With other asset choices, you must focus on whether to defer taxable income to the future and how to diversify realized income sources year over year. Therefore, whether you are a single senior or junior, you will be wise to work with a few key tax savings opportunities:

- *Protect earned income from tax erosion.* The best way to shelter current employment or self-employment income from tax is with the RRSP, which provides immediate tax savings and a tax deferral on investment income. An RRSP deduction is only available to those who are age eligible (under 72) and who have RRSP contribution room. For those over 71, continued tax sheltering in a Registered Retirement Income Fund (RRIF) or an annuity remains an option.

- *Earn tax efficient pension income sources.* There are few tax shelters for pension income—the government basically wants their tax dollar now—after providing years of deferrals to accumulations.

The pension income amount of up to $2,000 provides relief though. Who qualifies? Those who are:

– **Age 65 or older** and in receipt of pension payments from a superannuation plan, the taxable portions of foreign social security payments (less exempt amounts deducted on Line 256), and annuity payments from an RRSP, RRIF, or Deferred Profit Sharing Plan (DPSP)

– **Under age 65** and in receipt of periodic pensions as part of a life annuity or taxable portions of foreign social security payments. Annuity payments from an RRSP, RRIF or Deferred Profit Sharing Plan (DPSP) are only eligible if received as a result of the spouse's death.

As a result, singles bear a greater tax burden on pension income sources than households with couples do.

- *Relocate with tax caution.* Remember that the provincial taxes you pay will be determined by your province of residence on December 31. If you are moving from a province with lower rates than your next one, consider moving at the start of next year. If you move before

December 31 all income of the current year will be taxed at the new province's higher tax rates. Remember to check out a detailed list of moving expenses in *Essential Tax Fact Sheets* at www.knowledgebureau.com/ETF.

- *Be even more careful moving in.* Conjugal relationships can bring both positive and negative tax changes, including the following.
  - **On the positive side:** the opportunity to claim a spousal amount, transfer age, disability, pension or tuition, education and textbook amounts, share CPP benefits, split pension income, transfer dividend income (providing a spousal amount is increased or created by doing so), split other investment income sources (being mindful of the Attribution Rules), make a spousal RRSP contribution, and co-mingle medical expenses, political contributions or charitable donations to obtain a better net family claim.
  - **On the negative side:** the co-mingling of family net income will reduce claims for refundable credits and the loss of the amount for an eligible dependant. Also, as a family unit can only own one tax exempt principal residence, the gain on one will be taxable if two are owned.

Managing tax advantages of your first job

Feels good to have some cash, doesn't it? Most young singles don't realize that the time in life when you will have the most disposable income is often when you are a dependant, living at home and working at a good job. This is the time you should be saving, rather than spending... be sure to make a detailed list of Christmas and birthday wishes so that the other adults in your life can deal with non-deductible consumer spending needs on your behalf.

It pays handsomely to conform to four basic rules when you land your first job:

- Decide how much you are going to save and stick to this rule (50% if you can manage it is a great minimum number, especially if mom and dad are paying your living costs). Establish a Tax-Free Savings Account to shelter your investment income from taxes.

- Always file a tax return to build unused RRSP and Tax-Free Savings Account contribution room and tap into your GST Credit at age 19 (as a minimum file a tax return when you are 18 to tap into this).

- Always make your maximum RRSP contribution, based on available RRSP contribution room, when you become taxable (you can contribute before this and earn tax-deferred investment income, if you like, and save your deduction until later).

- Never overpay your taxes at source—make sure your employer is withholding the right amount of income tax, CPP and EI but no more. Remember if you are under 18, over 70 or in receipt of a CPP benefit, you don't need to contribute to the CPP. If your income is under $2,000 you will also qualify for a refund of EI contributions when you file your return.

The following income sources often earned by young singles also require special attention:

Essential TAX FACT #72

Report your tips or risk facing an expensive tax audit.

Essential TAX FACT #73

Employed apprentice mechanics may qualify for a tax deduction for the cost of their tools.

Essential TAX FACT #74

Students in receipt of scholarship, fellowship or bursary income will not be taxable on that income if they are eligible to claim the Tuition, Education and Textbook Amounts or relate to attending elementary or secondary school.

Waiter, bartenders and tips. If you work in the service industry as a waiter/ waitress, bellhop, taxi driver, etc. be sure to record tips received and report the amount on Line 104 of your income tax return. You may receive them in cash, but keep a log of your earnings, as audits are common in the hospitality industry. Without a daily record, the CRA may disagree with your income figures and increase them to the amount they decide they should be... especially if they audit the restaurant or check what your colleagues have been reporting as tips. You may elect to pay CPP contributions on your reported tips by filing *Form CPT20*.

Cost of tools. Special rules exist for new tool costs of tradespeople and apprentice vehicle mechanics. All tradespeople can deduct up to $500 of the cost of eligible tools in excess of $1,019 (for 2008). An additional deduction may be available for an apprentice motor vehicle mechanic.

Students and their scholastic rewards. If you are in receipt of a scholarship, fellowship or bursary, the income will be tax exempt if you otherwise qualify to claim an education amount. Scholarships that relate to attending elementary or secondary school are also tax exempt. If you don't qualify for the education amount, you'll be able to claim a $500 exemption. Similar prizes obtained through your employment, however, will not qualify for any exemption. If you are in receipt of a research grant, report only the net amount (amounts received less out of pocket expenses) on your tax return.

Remember to transfer any unused tuition, education and textbook amounts to your supporting parent, grandparent or spouse and to track any remaining amounts as well as unused student loan interest costs for carry forward. The interest credit can only be claimed by the student for interest paid on prescribed student loans made under the Canada Student Loans Act, the Canada Student Financial Assistance Act, or similar provincial or territorial government laws for post-secondary education. Unused claims can be carried forward for five years.

Leveraging investments: Pay down the mortgage or contribute to the RRSP?

When you buy a home, you will generally be taking a giant step towards wealth creation. This investment has the potential to provide you with:

1. Tax exempt capital appreciation

2. A hedge against future inflation

3. A possibility to produce income (from rentals or home office use)

4. Equity that can be leveraged to acquire other income-producing assets

Essential TAX FACT #75

Unused student loan interest may be carried forward for use by the student for up to 5 years.

Essential TAX FACT #76

Education Assistance Payments from RESPs are taxable to you when withdrawn. This will increase your net income, which could affect the size of your GST Credit and provincial tax credits. You may wish to make an RRSP contribution to offset this.

Essential TAX FACT #77

While capital gains enjoyed on the sale of your principal residence are not taxable, losses incurred are not tax deductible, either.

Buying a home can, however, provide some real risk as well. Aside from the taxes you pay throughout your lifetime, a mortgage on your home can be your most significant lifetime debt. The risk of loss is also present, especially if you have to move because you lose your job, are transferred, are getting divorced, or find the renewal of your mortgage brings with it substantially higher—and unaffordable—interest costs.

To make matters worse, losses on the sale of your personal residence are not tax deductible (although if you must sell because your employer requires you to move, the employer may be able to cushion your losses on a tax free basis. See the discussion of tax free benefits in Part Three).

Essential
TAX FACT #78

The cost of interest paid on your home mortgage is generally not tax deductible unless the home is used for an income-earning purpose by you as a self-employed individual.

Also significant is the fact that interest costs are usually non-deductible (however, if you use the home as an income-producing property, you may be able to write off a portion of those costs. See Part Five on revenue properties and Part Three on home office expenses.) Therefore you need to manage carefully the repayment of mortgage principal (the quicker the better) and mortgage interest payments (the lower the rate the better). Consider the following in your discussion on wealth creation and preservation with your advisors:

COMPARISON OF COSTS WITH VARYING DOWN PAYMENTS
$100,000 Home; 9% Interest Rate, Increased Down Payment of $25,000

Down Payment	Amortization	Monthly Payment	Total* P & I	Interest Only	Saving
$25,000	25 Years	$620.99	$186,297	$111,297	
$30,000	25 Years	$579.60	$173,880	$103,880	$ 7,417
$50,000	25 Years	$413.99	$124,197	$ 74,197	$37,100

*Principal and interest

By increasing your down payment by $25,000 up front, you'll save $37,100 in interest costs over 25 years.

COMPARISON OF COSTS WITH DIFFERENT AMORTIZATION PERIODS
Down payment of $25,000 on a $100,000 home, 9% interest rate

Amortization	Monthly Payment	Total P + I	Interest Only	Savings
25 years	$620.99	$186,297	$111,297	
15 years	$753.39	$135,610	$ 60,610	$50,687 over 25 years
10 years*	$943.42	$113,210	$ 38,210	$73,087 over 25 years

*By amortizing your mortgage over 10 years instead of 25, you will save close to $75,000 more towards your financial independence.

COMPARISON OF COSTS WITH INCREASING PAYMENT FREQUENCIES
$100,000 Home, $75,000 Mortgage at 9%, Original Amortization: 25 Years

Payment Frequency	Amount of Payment	Amortization	Interest	Savings
Monthly	$620.99	25 years	$111,297	
Accelerated Weekly*	$155.25	19.3 years	$80,642	$30,655

*Your monthly payment divided by 4 reaps significant savings by lopping almost 6 years off your amortization period. So if you can't afford a large down payment, compensate by making your mortgage payments every week instead of monthly.

Finally, your mortgage interest rate is the next most significant factor in managing your costs. The next chart shows how small differences in rates can multiply your cost savings:

COMPARISION OF COSTS WITH VARYING INTEREST RATES
$100,000 Home, $25,000 down payment; $75,000 Mortgage

Rate	Amortization	Monthly	Total* P + I	Interest Only	Savings over 10% rate
7%	25 Years	$525.32	$157,596	$ 82,596	$43,665
8%	25 Years	$572.42	$171,726	$ 96,726	$29,535
9%	25 Years	$620.99	$186,297	$111,297	$14,964
10%	25 Years	$670.87	$201,261	$126,261	n/a

*Assumes same rate and monthly payment throughout full amortization period. Figures are estimated.

COMPARISON OF COSTS WITH PREPAYMENTS OF PRINCIPAL
Original Amortization Period: 25 Years; on $75,000 mortgage at 9%
Prepayment of 20% of Mortgage in each of 5 years

Year	Monthly Payment	Balance Principal	Amortization Months	Interest Paid	Total Interest on life of mortgage
1	$620.99	$75,000	300	$6,593	$111,297
2	620.99	$59,313	166	$5,226	$ 50,364
3	620.99	$45,670	107	$4,110	$ 32,595
4	620.99	$33,862	70	$2,817	$ 25,536
5	620.99	$23,382	45	$2,204	$ 23,309

Here the result is that after the first five years, you have produced interest savings of $87,988 over what would have been paid under a 25 year amortization period. Not bad!

Obviously, the decision to buy your first home requires careful consideration around the level of your down payment, interest rates and monthly repayment schedule, which can make tens of thousands of dollars of difference to you in the long term. All of these factors should be discussed with your real estate advisor, tax professional, lawyer and financial institution.

But the burning question is this: how can I accumulate enough savings to do all of this in the first place? Your tax refund is a good place to start!

Assume you are in a 42% marginal tax bracket, and you contribute your maximum contribution to an RRSP this year, which your Notice of Assessment states is $12,000. Making the contribution will save you $5,040 on your tax return.

Now you take a look at your mortgage picture. Assume you will apply your tax savings, which you are receiving monthly because you have requested a reduction of taxes withheld at source, to your mortgage. This equates to $420 a month. If you have a $100,000 mortgage, currently amortized over 25 years, at an interest rate of 9%, you would be paying approximately $828 a month. If you bumped this payment up by $420, you'd cut your amortization period by almost 15 years. (Monthly payments of $1,248 on a $100,000 mortgage at 9% will pay it off in 10 years.)

Therefore by making your annual RRSP contribution you will create the following opportunity:

1. Accumulate tax sheltered earnings from principal of $12,000 for ten years. At a compounding rate of 9% this would grow to $198,724

2. Save 15 years on your mortgage amortization.
   25 years x $828 x 12 months   = $248,400
   10 years x ($828 + 420 = $1,248) x 12 months = $149,760
   Difference $98,640

3. Total accumulations by making annual RRSP contributions of $12,000 and investing them in the home mortgage over a 10 year period   = $297,364

The numbers speak for themselves!

Love and marriage: Integrate tax planning into new conjugal relationships

When you fall in love, and your single life turns to couplehood, it can be one of the most rewarding events of your life, not only for your emotional well being but also for your financial strength.

To start, your new living arrangements can generate a claim for the spousal amount. The spousal amount changes every year due to indexing. See www.knowledgebureau.com/ETF for more information. Provisions relating to the spousal amount relate equally to common-law partners. In each case, we are referring to unions between the same or opposite sex.

So when does one enter a conjugal (rather than platonic) living arrangement with a spouse for tax purposes? First, and simplest, is the act of legal marriage.

It is possible that you will be able to claim a "spousal amount" for your new wife or husband in the year of marriage, but this will be based on their net income (Line 236) for the whole year, no matter when you get married—even December 31!

If you choose to live as common-law partners, you will be treated the same as spouses for tax purposes if you live together as at the end of the year and you have a natural or adopted child together. If there is no child, once you have lived together for a continuous period of 12 months and in that time have not separated for more than 90 days you will attain common-law partner status.

It is also important to note that no taxpayer may claim the spousal amount in respect of more than one spouse or common-law partner in the year and that only one individual

Essential TAX FACT #79

You are considered to be spouses for tax purposes when you are legally married.

Essential TAX FACT #80

If spouses or common-law partners are living apart at the end of the taxation year, then only the spouse's income for the period while the couple were living together is used in the calculation of the spousal amount.

Essential TAX FACT #81

If one spouse is required to pay spousal support for the other spouse, in the year of change, the payor may either claim the spousal amount or take the deduction for spousal support paid, but not both.

Essential TAX FACT #82	

In the year of death, the spousal amount may be claimed in full on the final return or on any of the optional returns filed for the deceased.

Essential TAX FACT #83	

Gifts which enhance or supplement the already adequate lifestyle of a non-resident dependant do not constitute support.

may make the claim in respect of the other individual.

Where two (or more) individuals are qualified to make the claim in respect of another, they must agree who will be making the claim or neither will be allowed it.

A New Planning Tip. You should plan to take advantage of the opportunity to establish a TFSA for your new spouse, thereby avoiding the Attribution Rules on resulting investment earnings. This and spousal RRSP planning can help you accumulate new wealth as a couple.

Non-Resident Spouses. In order for you to claim the amount for a spouse or common-law partner who is a non-resident it is necessary that the spouse be supported by or be dependent on you. The question of support or dependency is determined on the facts of each case.

If the non-resident spouse or common-law partner has enough income or assistance for a reasonable standard of living in the country in which they live, they are not considered to be supported by or be dependent on you for support.

To support a claim for a non-resident spouse or common-law partner, you must provide proof of the amounts paid or given as support of the spouse or common-law partner.

Adoption Tax Credit. Taxpayers may claim a non-refundable tax credit for their eligible adoption expenses to a maximum of $10,643, a claim which may be split between adoptive parents. The claim is made in the year in which the adoption becomes finalized but may include expenses that were incurred in prior taxation years.

Single parents and their dependants

Whether you are a single parent by choice or circumstance, the tax system delivers three primary tax preferences to a single parent, which you should look into immediately after a baby is born:

- *Refundable credits.* Child Tax Benefits, Universal Child Care Benefits, Working Income Tax Benefit and GST Credits

- *Non-refundable credits.* Claims for the amount for eligible dependant, the amount for dependent children and the children's fitness amount

- *Deductions.* Claims for child care expenses

In addition, you should plan to save for your child's education immediately by tapping into generous tax-assisted savings provisions under the Registered Education Savings Plan (see Part Five). As a minimum, try to save the Universal Child Care Benefits and the Child Tax Benefits received in a separate account in the name of the child—resulting investment earnings will be taxed to the child rather than in your hands and therefore will accumulate on a tax free basis.

Claiming your tax credits. Both the federal and provincial governments provide tax credits to certain taxpayers to promote social and economic policy goals.

So just how do you claim these credits? The answer to the question is a bit mystical, as the majority of taxpayers have difficulty actually finding them on the tax return! Non-refundable tax credits are found on Schedule 1.

Most refundable tax credits are calculated automatically by CRA—so you don't normally see any forms or apply in any way to receive these credits,

Essential TAX FACT #84

Remember, the higher earning spouse may transfer and claim five of the spouse's available credits— the age, pension, tuition, textbook and education and disability amounts, and the amount for dependent children if the lower earner is not taxable. Co-mingling of medical, charitable and political expenses is allowed, as are contributions to a spousal RRSP. These are first steps to consider in tax planning within conjugal relationships.

Essential TAX FACT #85

Tax credits are tax preferences which are deducted from taxes owing or in some cases refunded to you, even if no taxes are owing. It is therefore important to understand your rights to "non-refundable" and "refundable" credits.

other than by filing your personal income tax return.

Another point of confusion for tax filers is how tax credits differ from tax deductions. Non-refundable tax credits provide equal benefits to all taxpayers, whereas tax deductions benefit taxpayers in higher tax brackets more than taxpayers in lower tax brackets. However, certain refundable and non-refundable tax credits are determined in conjunction with a net income-based means test. That is, some credits are "clawed back" when income exceeds a certain pre-determined level, thereby phasing out benefits to higher income earners. Unfortunately, this results in higher marginal tax rates for those within these "clawback zones" than for the highest income earners.

Also note that non-refundable credits found on Schedule 1 are of no benefit to those with no taxes owing.

The Child Tax Benefit. This federal refundable tax credit is composed of the National Child Tax Benefit and two supplements, the National Child Tax Benefit Supplement for lower-income families and the Child Disability Benefit for families with disabled children. Certain provinces and territories also offer child benefit and credit programs administered by CRA.

The CTB is paid each month to an eligible individual for a qualified dependant, who is a person who was:

- under 18

- not claimed as a spouse or common-law partner by another individual

The recipient of the benefit must also:

- reside with the qualified dependant
- be the parent who is primarily responsible for the care and upbringing of the qualified dependant (the female parent who lives with the child is generally considered to be that person)
- be a resident of Canada or the spouse or common-law partner of a resident of Canada

The amounts paid monthly are calculated for a "benefit year"; that is, the period July 1 to June 30. The level of benefits is based on the net family income reported by the parents for the tax year ending before the benefit year.

Essential TAX FACT #88

Once eligibility for the Child Tax Benefit is established, both the eligible individual and the spouse or common-law partner must file an income tax return each year to maintain eligibility. If the spouse or common-law partner is a non-resident, *Form CTB9* must be filed to report their income.

When the family situation changes, that is the parent marries, starts living common-law, separates or divorces, CRA should be notified as soon as possible so that the correct family net income can be taken into account in the calculation of the next child tax benefit amount. Use form RC65 to notify CRA of such changes in marital status.

The Child Tax Benefit has several lucrative components you may qualify to receive:

- *The National Child Tax Benefit.* This consists of a basic amount plus an additional amount for the third and subsequent dependants.

  The National Child Tax Benefit Supplement. This is an additional payment for the first child, the second child, and for the third and subsequent children. The annual amount is reduced by a different percentage of the family net income in excess of a base amount, depending on the number of dependants.

- *The Canada Learning Bond.* This is a new notional account which will be payable to parents of children born after 2003 who are eligible for the National Child Tax Benefit Supplement. It allows for an enhanced Canada Education Savings Grant for low income earners who invest money in an RESP for their child. See Part Five for more information.

- *The Child Disability Benefit.* This special amount is paid for each qualified dependant who is eligible for the disability amount.

The Child Tax Benefit is one of the most lucrative provisions in the Income Tax Act for Canadian children. Be sure you maximize it by keeping an eagle eye on the size of your net income (try to keep it below income-testing thresholds with an RRSP deposit. See *Essential Tax Fact Sheets* at www.knowledgebureau.com/ETF for income limit details.)

**Essential
TAX FACT #89**

The $100 per month Universal Child Care Benefit must be reported as income by the spouse or common-law partner with the lower net income.

The Universal Child Care Benefit (UCCB). If you are eligible to receive the Child Tax Benefit you are also eligible to receive a new benefit of $100 per month for each child under the age of 6 years (for the purposes of reducing child care costs). The UCCB does not depend on your income level so if you do not receive the CTB because your family net income is too high you are still eligible to receive the UCCB. To apply for the benefit use *Form RC66 Canada Child Tax Benefit Application*. If your spouse or common-law partner is a non-resident, *Form CTB9 Canada Child Tax Benefit Statement* must be filed to report their income.

This benefit must be reported as income (on line 117) by the lower-income spouse or common-law partner. Thus, if both spouses work, the income will be taxable at the marginal rate of the lower-income spouse. For families where the higher-income spouse claims an amount for the lower-income spouse, the UCCB will be taxed at the lowest tax rate.

Although taxable, the UCCB is not to be taken into account for the purposes of calculating income-tested benefits delivered through the income tax system such as the Child Tax Benefit and GST Credit (see below). Receipt of the UCCB will also not increase the clawback of Employment Insurance or Old Age Security benefits.

**Essential
TAX FACT #90**

If the total GSTC for the year exceeds $100 then one-quarter of the amount will be paid in July, October, January, and April. If the total credit is $100 or less, it is paid in July.

The UCCB does not affect the amount that may be claimed for Child Care Expenses.

The Goods and Services Tax Credit. Similar to the CTB, the GSTC is not considered to be income to the recipient. Rather it is a way to reimburse low earners, who must pay the Goods and Services Tax, which is levied on consumption rather than ability to pay.

The GST/HST Credit is paid quarterly to eligible individuals in respect of themselves, their spouses or common-law partners and qualified dependants. It is based on the family income reported on the income tax return for the year ending before the July 1 benefit year. Note that if the taxpayer has a balance due to CRA, the GST/HST credit may be applied to such outstanding taxes.

Who is eligible to receive it? This is someone who in a particular payment quarter:

- is at least 19 years old at the beginning of the quarter,
- was a parent who resided with their child, or
- was in a marriage or common-law partnership.

Where two eligible individuals are cohabiting spouses or common-law partners then only one of the eligible individuals may apply for the GST/HST Credit.

A qualified dependant for GSTC purposes is a person who:

- is the child of the individual or dependent for support on the individual or the individual's spouse or common-law partner
- resides with the individual
- is under 19 year of age

The following individuals will not receive the GSTC:

- deceased individuals
- persons confined to a prison for at least 90 days which includes the first day of the quarter.
- persons for whom a special allowance under the *Children's Special Allowances Act* is paid

Essential TAX FACT #91

Because an individual will become eligible in the quarter following the 19th birthday, it is important that 18-year olds file an income tax return.

Essential TAX FACT #92

Individuals who become residents of Canada in the year should file *Form RC151* to apply for the GST/HST Credit. The credit will be paid starting the quarter after the individual becomes a Canadian resident.

Essential TAX FACT #93

If the marital status of an eligible individual changes, CRA should be notified either by letter or using *Form RC65*.

- non-residents, except those who are married or living common-law with a resident of Canada or who were a resident before the quarter.

To apply for the Goods and Services/Harmonized Sales Tax Credit, mark the box labelled "Yes" next to the question "Are you applying for the GST/HST credit?" on page 1 of the T1 return.

In 2007 a new credit was introduced for low income taxpayers who have employment or self-employment income—the Working Income Tax Benefit (WITB). In order to qualify, you must be a resident in Canada and you must not have been a full-time student or in prison. Note the following essential facts:

- The WITB is calculated as 20% of earned income in excess of $3,000.

- Earned income is the total of employment and business income for the year (ignoring losses).

- In most provinces it is clawed back when net family income exceeds $9,681 (single taxpayer) or $14,776 (family or single parent). Rates vary in BC, Quebec, and Nunavut.

- Net income for purposes of the clawback is calculated in exactly the same way as it is for the Universal Child Care Benefit.

- The WITB may be claimed by either spouse (or common-law partner) but only one spouse may make a claim for the family.

- You must apply by filing the form included in your tax return package.

See Essential Tax Fact Sheets at www.knowledgebureau.com/ETF for more information.

A Special Non-Refundable Tax Credit for Single Parents. Singles should also be interested in a particular non-refundable tax credit available if there is a child in the family. This is known as the Amount for anEligible Dependant and it brings an "equivalent-spouse amount" into the family, based on the dependant's net income.

The credit is found first on Schedule 5 and is transferred to Schedule 1 of the tax return, line 305. It is available if you did not claim the spouse or common-law partner amount and:

- you were not married or living common-law or
- you were married or living common-law but
  - did not live with a spouse or common-law partner and
  - did not support or were not supported by a spouse or common-law partner

and you support and live with a dependant in a home which you maintain. To qualify, the dependant must be:

- your child,
- your parent or grandparent, or
- under 18 years of age or wholly dependent on you because of mental or physical infirmity.

These qualifications need not be met throughout the year but must be met at some time during the year. In addition the following rules must be observed:

- Only one person can claim the amount for an eligible dependant in respect of the same dependant.
- No one may claim the amount for an eligible dependant if someone else is claiming the amount for spouse or common-law partner for that dependant.
- Only one claim may be made for the amount for an eligible dependant for the same home. Where more than one taxpayer qualifies to make the claim, the taxpayers must agree who will make the claim or no one will be allowed to.
- If a claim for the amount for an eligible dependant is made in respect of a dependant, no one may claim the amount for infirm dependants or the caregiver amount in respect of the same dependant.

Child Care: A Special Tax Deduction for Working Parents. When you have a child, it is quite likely you may at some point have to pay child care expenses while you work or go to school. Eligible expenses will be claimed as a deduction on the tax return and will reduce your net income—which in turn can increase the refundable tax credits we discussed above. Please see *Essential Tax Fact Sheets* at www.knowledgebureau.com/ETF for details of the child care expense claim.

Claim for Dependent Children. If you have children under 18 living at home, you can claim a non-refundable credit of $2,038 for each child. This new credit is not reduced if the child has income. Where custody is shared, only one parent may make the claim for each child. Where one parent is claiming the child as an eligible dependant, only that parent may also make the claim for that child as a minor dependant.

Essential
TAX FACT #95

The Income Tax Act allows for a tax-free rollover of capital assets to a former spouse on breakdown of the marriage.

Essential
TAX FACT #96

Upon relationship breakdown, spouses may elect that gains or losses realized on the disposition of capital property transferred while the taxpayers are living apart should not be allocated back to the other spouse or common-law partner.

Essential
TAX FACT #97

The minimum holding period requirement is not observed on spousal RRSPs when the taxpayers are living apart as a result of a breakdown in their relationship.

Suddenly single again: Planning tax-wise exits

When spouses or common-law partners have lived apart for a period of at least 90 days because of a breakdown of their conjugal relationship, then from the beginning of that 90-day period they are no longer treated as spouses.

In the year of such a breakdown, there are numerous significant tax rules to observe including:

- the division of assets
- spousal or common-law partner RRSPs
- the claiming of child care expenses
- support payments made and received
- legal fees paid
- federal non-refundable credits such as claims for dependent children under the dependent child amount and the amount for eligible dependants and refundable credits including the Child Tax Benefit, Universal Child Care Benefit, and the Working Income Tax Benefit, and
- provincial credits.

Division of assets. On the breakdown of a marriage or common-law relationship, where the terms of a separation or divorce agreement require that the funds from one spouse's DPSP, RESP, RPP, RRSP, or RRIF be transferred to the other, the funds may be transferred on a tax free basis.

Cost of transferred property. The transfer of depreciable property between spouses as a result of a relationship breakdown takes place at the Undepreciated Capital Cost of the property. As a result, no recapture, terminal loss, or capital gain is incurred on the transfer. For other property, the transfer takes place at the Adjusted Cost Base of the assets.

Attribution rules. When one spouse transfers assets to the other, the Attribution Rules generally attribute any income earned by the transferred assets back to the transferor. However the Attribution Rules do not apply to income earned during the period when the former spouses are living apart because of a breakdown in the relationship. Capital gains or losses continue to attribute back unless the spouses elect otherwise.

Essential TAX FACT #98

Alimony or support payments made to a spouse or common-law partner are taxable to the recipient and deductible by the payor. In the year of separation or divorce, however, the payer may claim either the deduction for support or the spousal amount, but not both.

Spousal RRSPs. Withdrawals from spousal or common-law partner RRSPs made by the annuitant are generally reportable by the contributing spouse if any RRSP contribution has been made in the current year or the previous two years. However, this rule is waived for separated/divorced couples.

Child care expenses. Child care expenses must normally be claimed by the lower income spouse but may be claimed by the higher income spouse during a period where the taxpayer was separated from the other supporting person due to a breakdown in their relationship for a period of at least 90 days as long as they were reconciled within the first 60 days after the taxation year. If the taxpayers were not reconciled within 60 days after the taxation year, then each spouse may claim any child care expenses they paid during the year with no adjustment for child care expenses claimed by the other taxpayer.

Legal fees on separation or divorce. Legal fees to obtain a divorce or separation agreement are normally not deductible. However, as of October 10, 2002, CRA considers legal costs incurred to obtain spousal support relating specifically to the care of children (not the spouse) under the Divorce Act or under provincial legislation, as well as the costs incurred to obtain an increase in support or make child support non-taxable, to be deductible.

Federal refundable tax credits. The Child Tax Benefit (CTB) and Goods and Services Tax Credit (GSTC) are forward-looking amounts. That is, they are received as a redistribution of income for the purpose of assistance with the current expenses of mid and low income earners in the next "benefit year"—July to June, but they are calculated based on net family income from the prior tax year.

Essential TAX FACT #99

When a family break-down occurs, CRA should be immediately notified so that the calculation of the credits for the next CTB or GSTC payment may be made without including the estranged spouse or common-law partner's net income.

Immediate notification of change in marital status is most important to supplement monthly income, especially in the case of the CTB. Also, be sure to do so because the statute of limitations for recovery of missed or underpaid credits is generally only 11 months, although some leniency may be available.

The Income Tax Act assumes that the eligible CTB recipient is the female parent. However, "prescribed factors" will be considered in determining what constitutes care and upbringing and who is fulfilling that responsibility.

For example, where, after the breakdown of a conjugal relationship, the single parent and child returns to live with his or her parents, the single parent will continue to be presumed to be the supporting individual unless they too are under 18 years old. In that case, the grandparents may claim the Child Tax Benefit for both their child and their grandchild.

Provincial Tax Credits. Many provinces have tax reductions or refundable credits that are based on family net income. In most cases, in the year of separation, it is not necessary to include the estranged spouse or common-law partner's income in the family income calculation and normally no credits or reductions on behalf of the estranged spouse or common-law partner will be allowed. Each partner will claim the credits or reductions to which he or she is entitled.

Singles who give care to dependent adults

It is possible to be single and give care, either alone or in conjunction with other caregivers. For example, two single siblings could be sharing the care of an aging, disabled parent. In that case, the Income Tax Act allows for the splitting of certain non-refundable tax credits. The significant credits you should be familiar with are:

Amount for eligible dependants. As discussed under Single Parents, if you do not have a spouse or common-law partner but maintained a dwelling in Canada and supported a person related by blood, marriage or adoption who was under 18 and lived with you in that dwelling you may claim the Amount for an Eligible Dependant (formally know as the Equivalent-to-Spouse amount). Only one claim may be made for each dwelling and for each dependant.

Essential TAX FACT #100

If you are single, you may wish to claim an Amount for Eligible Dependant or the Caregiver Amount, whichever yields a better overall result. Claims can be split between caregivers, provided that the total amount claimed for the same dependant does not exceed one full claim.

Amount of infirm dependants 18 and over. If you support a dependant who is 18 and over and mentally or physically infirm, a special credit is available based on that dependant's net income level. This will include income from Old Age Security, Guaranteed Income Supplements, Spouse's Allowances, CPP benefits, EI Benefits, Workers' Compensation Payments and Social Assistance. Members of your extended family may qualify—parents, grandparents, siblings, aunts, uncles, nephews, nieces, and in-laws—if infirm and living in Canada.

Caregiver Amount. If you care for an elderly parent or grandparent or other disabled dependant who is over 17 years old and living with you in your home, you may be eligible to claim the Caregiver Amount. This claim is also based on the dependant's net income, but is phased out at higher income threshold levels, making it possible to make a claim even if the dependant is receiving Old Age Security and Canada Pension Plan income. If a claim for an Amount for an Eligible Dependant was also made for this dependant, the Caregiver Amount will be reduced by that claim.

Essential TAX FACT #101

The Caregiver Amount will not be claimable unless the dependant is living with you—even if you provide substantially all supports to your dependant in their home.

Disability Amount. This is possibly one of the most lucrative yet most frequently missed provisions on the tax return. It requires the signing of a form by a medical practitioner—*Form T2201 Disability Tax Credit Certificate.*

Please read Tax Fact #102. Note, if a person was diagnosed with cancer in September and the condition of the disease became debilitating by the end of the year, the amount would be claimable for the whole year.

The condition must "markedly restrict" the patient. Examples are:

- blindness at any time in the year

- inability to feed or dress oneself (or situations in which this is possible but only after taking an inordinately long period of time to do so)

- inability to perform basic functions, even with therapy or the use of devices and medication. These can include:
  - perceiving, thinking, remembering or other cognitive functions
  - speaking to be understood by a familiar person in a quiet setting
  - hearing to understand a familiar person in a quiet setting
  - walking
  - controlling bowel and/or bladder functions

In addition, those persons who receive therapy to support a vital function—like kidney dialysis—for an average of at least 14 hours a week will qualify to claim this credit. A supplement is available for those who support disabled children. However, if child care expenses are claimed for the child, the supplement will be reduced. Prior to 2005, an individual's impairments were evaluated separately. Beginning in 2006, individuals who suffer from multiple restrictions that together have an impact on their everyday lives may also be eligible to claim the disability amount.

If the amount is not needed by the disabled person because that person is not taxable, the amount can be transferred to a supporting individual. If that person is a spouse, use Schedule 2; otherwise a special line is allocated for transfers from other dependants: Line 318. There are some special rules in making this claim to take note of, however:

- the Disability Amount and the Disability Supports Deduction may both be claimed on the tax return. However, that deduction could limit the disability amount supplement claimed for minor children.

- you cannot claim both the costs of nursing home care or full time attendant care as a medical expense and the Disability Amount. One or the other can be claimed but not both.

- those who pay someone to come into the home to provide care for the sick may claim expenditures up to $10,000 ($20,000 in the year of death) and still claim the Disability Amount.

Note: Consider investing in the Registered Disability Savings Plan for disabled dependants in your life. The RDSP allows for leveraging of individual contributions through government contributions to the plan. See Part One for more details.

Rules for claiming medical expenses

The claim for medical expenses is one of the most common provisions on the return—it affects the majority of tax filers—yet it is most often under-claimed and misunderstood.

Medical expenses may be claimed for:

- you, your spouse or common-law partner;

- a child or grandchild of you or your spouse who depended on you for support, and

- adult children or grandchildren, a parent, grandparent, brother, sister, uncle, aunt, niece, or nephew of you or your spouse who lived in Canada at any time in the year and depended on you for support.

In the case of expenditures for the first two groups of dependants, the total medical expenses are co-mingled and then reduced by 3% of your net income. The claim is made at Line 330 of the tax return. It is generally to your advantage to claim the medical expenses for these individuals on the return of the lower-income family member, because of this limitation, unless that person is not taxable.

Essential TAX FACT #103

Medical expenses can be claimed for the best 12-month period ending in the tax year. Medical expenses should be grouped in a twelve month period that bears the best claim. This could be February 1 to January 31, May 1 to April 30 and so on.

Essential TAX FACT #104

In the year of death, the normal 12-month period for making the medical expense claim is increased to a 24-month period that includes the date of death. Medical expenses paid by the executor after death may be included.

Medical expenses for dependent adults may be added to the return of a supporting individual, but that claim is calculated separately on Line 331 of the return. Total medical expenses must be reduced by 3% of the dependant's net income and the maximum claim under this category is $10,000, applied separately to each individual claimed here. The claim must be for the same 12 month period chosen for medical expenses made at Line 330.

Note that starting in 2008, new medical expenses claimable include:

(a) for those who have severe autism or epilepsy, these expenses :

- the cost of acquiring, caring for and maintaining an animal to assist the taxpayer
- travel, board and lodging expenses for attending a school or other facility for training in the use and handling of such animals.

(b) various new devices including:

- altered auditory feedback devices for those with speech impairments
- electrotherapy devices designed to be used by a person with a medical condition or a severe mobility impairment
- standing devices designed for those with a severe mobility impairment to undertake standing therapy
- pressure pulse therapy devices designed for use by those with balance disorders

Essential TAX FACT #106

As long as you are a resident of Canada, medical expenses incurred abroad are also claimable, including Blue Cross and other travel or private health insurance premiums.

Allowable medical expenditures. See *Essential Tax Fact Sheets* at www.knowledge-bureau.com/ETF for a list of allowable payments to medical practitioners, or for treatments and devices.

Blue Cross and similar private health insurance premiums are often deducted by the employer; the amount paid by the employer and included in the employee's income will be shown on the T4 slip; amounts paid by the employee will likely be shown on pay stubs.

Note, when travelling to receive medical services, actual receipts can be used for costs of travel including gas, hotel and meals, or you can claim vehicle expenses using a simplified method based on a rate per kilometre. This method does not require receipts to be kept for vehicle expenses, only a record of the number of kilometres driven. If you are travelling from one province to another for treatment, the rate is calculated based on the province in which the trip began. For ongoing current rates, visit the CRA web site at: http://www.cra-arc.gc.ca/travelcosts.

Practice strategic philanthropy

Most Canadians give to charities at some point in the year. Those gifts, usually of money, will be claimed on the tax return, first on *Schedule 9 Donations and Gifts*, and then on *Schedule 1*. The amounts donated to Registered Canadian Charities must be supported by receipts that have official registration numbers.

The claim for donations is a two-tiered federal credit: 15% on the first $200 and 29% on the balance. The real dollar value is higher than this, when provincial taxes are factored in. Because the rate is higher on donations over $200, it may be advantageous to group donations between spouses, or common-law partners who are allowed to claim each other's donations. You may carry forward donations for up to five years, for a better claim.

Note that there are special lucrative tax rules for those who transfer publicly traded shares to their favorite charity or private foundation.

Starting in 2006 the capital gains inclusion rate for the donation of publicly traded securities to a registered charity was reduced to nil. Parallel changes effectively removed from employment income the net taxable portion of the

**Essential
TAX FACT #107**

You may claim travel expenses for the patient and one attendant who must travel 40 km or more to receive medical services not available in your community; additional costs may be claimed when travelling 80 km or more.

**Essential
TAX FACT #108**

A transfer of shares of a private Canadian controlled corporation to a charity is ignored at the time of the donation. The donation credit is claimed if the security is disposed of within five years. This includes disposition by death of donor; however, the donations credit will be allowed at that time if the donor dies before the five-year period is up.

gain on the exercise of a stock option where the employee donated the shares to a charity.

Gifts made on or after March 19, 2007 to a private foundation will also qualify for the zero inclusion rate.

The February 26, 2008 federal budget extended the current capital gains exemption on the donation of publicly-traded securities to include capital gains on the exchange of unlisted securities that are donated within 30 days of an exchange for publicly traded securities. This will include exchanges after February 26, 2008 of a partnership interest or shares in a private corporation for publicly traded shares if these shares are donated to a qualified donee within 30 days of the exchange.

Therefore taxpayers will receive an advantage in earning tax exempt capital gains and a donation receipt when qualifying investments are donated.

CHAPTER REFLECTION:
ESSENTIAL TAX FACTS FOR SINGLES AND SENIORS

Special tax provisions are available for junior and senior singles who are humming along just fine on their own, or providing loving care and support to dependants around them. Modern lifestyles and demographic challenges drive tax change, and so it is important for you to be aware and make the tax system work for you in whatever part of your lifecycle you find yourself. Ask your tax and financial advisors about the tax provisions available.

For Those Who Live Alone

- Maximization of income diversification and deferral options
- Creation of tax exempt and tax efficient asset holdings
- Retirement income planning strategies in the absence of income splitting opportunities
- Maximization of tax deductible spousal support and legal fees
- Charitable donation strategies for estate planning

- Maximization of non-refundable credits:
  - overpayments of source deductions for CPP and EI
  - the age amount (for those age 65 and older)
  - qualifying pension income amount (for those who receive private pension income)
  - the disability amount
  - medical expenses
- Maximization of refundable tax credits:
  - the GSTC and WITB as well as provincial tax credits
  - medical expenses supplement (only if there is earned income from employment or self-employment).

For Those Who Care for a Spouse or Common-Law Partner or Former Partner

- Consider conjugal or marital status if reconciliation takes place

- Seniors consider splitting qualifying pension income

- If providing care to a sick spouse or common-law partner, be sure to consider claiming:
  - the spousal amount
  - transfer minor child amount
  - public transit amounts
  - transfer of the spouse's age, disability, pension or tuition, education and textbook amounts
  - medical expenses and charitable donations as well as political contributions made by spouse
  - medical expense supplement—but only if there is income from employment or self-employment sources.

For Single Parents, in Addition to Some of the Provisions Above

- Consider the reporting of taxable support payments and the requirement to make instalment payments

- Use the RRSP deduction to increase refundable and non-refundable tax credits

- Claim child care expenses

- Claim the amount for eligible dependant

- Claim the amount for dependent children Children's Fitness Amount
- Plan for refundable tax credits, in particular the Child Tax Benefit and Universal Child Care Benefit
- Make RESP and RDSP deposits.

For Those Who Care for Other Relatives

If you are providing care to other relatives who are sick, your advisor will be claiming the following credits and asking you for supporting documents:

- The amount for infirm dependants age 18 and older
- The caregiver amount
- Medical expenses for that dependant
- Make RDSP deposits if relative is disability tax credit-eligible.
- Consider making TFSA (Tax-Free Savings Account) deposits for anyone who wishes to/needs to build wealth on a tax exempt basis.

NOW PUT MORE MONEY IN YOUR POCKET ALL YEAR LONG...

PERSPECTIVE

Single taxpayers—students, moms or dads, widows or widowers, the separated or divorced—all have unique opportunities under the Canadian tax system. While they miss out on provisions like pension income splitting later in life, they are able to take advantage of certain non-refundable tax credits which put them at least on par with those who live in conjugal relationships. In addition, because only one net family income is considered, refundable tax credits are often more lucrative for singles.

Still, it remains that the biggest challenge for many singles is wealth accumulation and preservation. Because everyone has the potential of being single not just once, but several times in life, it is important to be tax efficient early and consistently to enable self sufficiency and independence during periods of singlehood, and in retirement. It can really help to learn some basic investing skills, and endeavor to acquire a tax exempt principal residence.

PART FIVE

ESSENTIAL TAX FACTS
FOR NEW INVESTORS

What's important?

In these volatile times of change, every investor is a new investor. Think about it: unprecedented fluctuations in stock prices, changing currency valuations, a Canadian boomer demographic that is affluent, educated, but approaching pensionable age, and new investments to take into consideration all make this a time when peak personal productivity meets the power of a properly constructed and managed portfolio of investments.

In short, the rubber is hitting the road when it comes to actual, investment results for many Canadians who now need to count on their accumulated wealth to create enough income to fund the transition to a post-work stage.

This year, two new investments have stepped onto the stage: The Tax-Free Savings Account (TFSA) and Registered Disability Savings Plan (RDSP) to help families save on a tax exempt and tax preferred basis. That's some of the only good news to have emerged in the past year for investors.

Most Canadians who understand the value of their affluence, know that the biggest eroder of their wealth will likely be taxation. Yet few have taken direct steps to reducing their lifetime tax bill at this critical juncture. It requires a review of how individual investments are going to be taxed on withdrawal, and this Part of Essential Tax Facts is dedicated to just that.

So if you are at the front end of an investment savings cycle, remember, it just doesn't make sense to use the tax return as a savings vehicle! Rather, always maximize your opportunity to arrange your affairs within the framework of the law to pay the least amount of tax possible—throughout your lifetime—so that you can use those accumulations to have fun after work!

Please read the following pages with this in mind, and a view to answering the following key questions:

1. How do you use the time value of money to efficiently build after-tax wealth?

2. What are the six key strategies required to build a million-dollar portfolio?

3. How do funds invested in registered savings plans help you increase tax savings?

4. How does the new Tax-Free Savings Account work?

5. How do RRSP contributions increase your refundable tax credits?

6. What is the maximum dollar limit for RRSP contributions this year?

7. What is your maximum age eligibility for making RRSP contributions?

8. How does a spousal RRSP work?

9. What are the tax consequences of making an investment in a non-registered account?

10. How does income from property differ from income of a business for tax purposes?

11. How is interest income reported, and what marginal tax rates apply to this?

12. How can you benefit from tax advantages in your accrued capital gains and losses?

13. How can dividend income be used to lower your overall tax burden?

14. Can you do more to maximize the write-offs from your revenue properties?

15. How can you save more for family members in investment and education accounts?

16. Despite the write off for carrying charges, is leveraging your capital asset base the right thing to do?

What's new?

The best news for investors for some time is the new Tax-Free Savings Account. Beginning in 2009, taxpayers who are over 17 will earn $5000 each year in contribution room to their TFSA. That means that in 2009, you'll be able to contribute up to $5000 to a TFSA and any income earned on those contributions will not be taxable—ever. Then in 2010, you'll be able to contribute another $5,000 (to be indexed each year in $500 increments based on changes to Consumer Price Index). If you didn't make your 2009 contribution in full, you'll be able to contribute the $5,000 for 2010, plus any of the 2009 contribution room that you did not use.

While the immediate tax savings for a TFSA are not as great as for an RRSP, this is a great opportunity for those who cannot contribute to an RRSP because they don't have contribution room. In the long term, the TFSA contribution may be more lucrative than the RRSP contribution because the RRSP contribution, plus accumulated earnings will all be taxable. The TFSA contribution and earnings will all be tax-free when removed. Moreover, if you have to remove your TFSA accumulations for emergency purposes, you'll be able to put that money back with no tax consequences—unlike your RRSP when you can only put the money back if you have new RRSP contribution room.

Check out Part One of this book and the explanations that follow for these new items of interest for new investors:

- The RDSP
- The TFSA
- New RRSP Maximum Dollar Contributions
- Changes for RESP Contributors

Saving the first, not the last dollar

For many people, the filing of their tax return is the most significant financial transaction of the year. It's deadline-driven, comes with the threat of rather expensive consequences for non-compliance, and forces you to take an annual glance at your financial affairs—a kind of "financial physical", if you will.

Working and saving money are all the more meaningful when you apply all available tax preferences to basic money management techniques. That is, by combining the time value of money with tax-efficient investing, family income splitting and "tax cost averaging", you'll multiply your economic efforts and accumulate more wealth.

What do we mean by "the time value of money"? The concept is simple: a dollar in your pocket today is more valuable than a dollar to be received in the future. When you compute present value, you calculate what your cash flow in the future will be worth in today's dollars. When you calculate future value, you determine how large an investment today will grow to be in the future.

It is important to understand both the present and future value of every dollar you earn. You can make today's dollar work for you immediately by investing it…but only if it is in your possession in the first place. That's why you need to plan to take home more of the first dollars you make by being vigilant about tax overpayments at source. In a perfect world, each extra dollar should then be invested with a view to cutting taxes even further now, and all year long!

Too good to be true? Not at all—it's possible to have your cake and eat it too, when it comes to tax-efficient capital accumulation. But you've just got to believe…in the discipline of saving your money. You can do it! Accumulating capital is so motivating, when you "get the numbers".

Invest now to accumulate the most

The future value of the assets you invest today can be projected by combining the time period until the investment matures, the rate of return, inflation and the impact of taxes. Consider the following:

Unless you write savings directly into your budget, you likely won't have any. It doesn't have to be much, just be sure you write it in. Start with a reasonable goal…$1,000 a year. That's $2.74 cents a day, or $19.23 a week, or $83.33 a month. How much money will you have if you save $2.75, every day until you retire?

Age Today	Years to Age 65	Capital Saved
25	40	$40,150
35	30	$30,113
45	20	$20,075

Now consider what a difference starting early can make. The following shows the investment of $1,000 a year at an annual compounding rate of 10%:

A. Invests $1,000 a year for 10 years starting at age 20		B. Invests $1,000 a year starting at age 30	
Age	Accumulations	Age	Accumulations
20	$ 1,000	20	nil
30	$ 17,531	30	$ 1,000
40	$ 45,471	40	$18,531
50	$117,941	50	$64,003
Total Capital Invested: $10,000		Total Capital Invested: $21,000	

Even though Investor A invested less than half as much capital, s/he ends up with over twice as much at the end of a 40 year period. It pays to save first, party later.

Finally, add the power of tax sheltering to your $1,000 at an annual compounding rate of 10%, and the results are even more astounding:

Years	Value of Investment Outside RRSP Principal in After Tax Dollars: $720 Assuming a 28% tax rate	Value of an Investment inside RRSP, Principal in Pre-Tax Dollars: $1,000; or inside TFSA, Principal in After Tax Dollars: $720
10	$ 13,342	$ 18,531
20	$ 46,082	$ 64,003
30	$130,999	$181,943
40	$351,253	$487,852

By investing in a Tax-Free Savings Account, you'll save the taxes on the earnings in the account each year, which means your savings will compound much more quickly. Your TFSA contribution does more than just earn tax sheltered income. It has actually created new tax free capital for you by eliminating your taxes payable on this source. As a result of this, your social benefits are also unaffected as you will realize no increase in your family net income with the TFSA. Your effective marginal tax benefits could be well over 50%, depending on your income bracket. That's a great return for your money...

Inflation erodes the purchasing power of your dollar. At an inflation rate of 2%, the future value of $1.00 today will be 67 cents in 20 years. That means the purchasing power of $500,000 in savings will be about $334,000. Yikes! You'll need to protect every dollar you earn even more...and one way to do this is by looking out for the best real rates of return over time, taking into account both inflation and taxes. Ask your financial advisors about this.

So, if you really want to be a millionaire some day, you'll start saving now and in the process, prioritize how you will best use your time and money:

- Don't overpay taxes at source (withholding or instalment).

- Keep an emergency fund on hand in a non-registered account.

- Look for the best rates of investment return after inflation and taxes.

- Keep credit card balances down (don't give away high rates of return to your credit card company especially since they are generally not tax deductible).

- Remember: not all income sources are taxed alike: choose a tax efficient income mix in your non-registered investment accounts.

- Always make your RRSP contribution and if you don't have RRSP contribution room, contribute to a TFSA instead.

Create new capital quickly:
Contribute to a registered savings account

If you are a new investor, the first thing you're likely to be asked when you're opening a savings account is this: will you be opening a registered or non-registered account with us?

Investments held in a "registered account" will have the following characteristics:

- Investment income earned on the principal will be tax deferred until withdrawal. This allows capital to compound faster than if tax were paid along the way.

- The deposit may produce a tax deduction for the principal invested. The prime example is the Registered Retirement Savings Plan (RRSP), which is based on your unused RRSP contribution room, as calculated by the CRA. That's great for you, because this type of investment creates new dollars for investment purposes by reducing your taxes payable and often increasing social benefits available through the tax system. Also, investment income earned within the RRSP is tax deferred until withdrawal.

- Another registered investment that produces a tax deduction is the Registered Pension Plan (RPP) which is a company sponsored plan funded by contributions of the employer and employee. Income earned within that plan is also tax deferred.

- Some registered plans don't produce a deduction, but feature tax-sheltered income earning opportunities. These include the new Tax-Free Savings Account (TFSA), Registered Education Savings Plans (RESPs) and Registered Disability Savings Plans (RDSPs), which we will discuss in more detail in the later chapters, and Deferred Profit Sharing Plans (DPSPs).

**Essential
TAX FACT #110**

Your net income on Line 236 of the return will be reduced by your deduction for RPP and RRSP contributions.

**Essential
TAX FACT #111**

When your investment earnings compound on a tax-deferred basis within a registered account, you tap into the most tax efficient way to earn investment income.

- When accumulations within a registered plan are later withdrawn for your use, earnings are added to income in full for all plans except the TFSA. If you were able to deduct the contributions (RRSPs and RPPs) then the principal is also added to your income.

Maximize opportunities with the new Tax-Free Savings Account

Beginning in 2009, everyone who is over 17 and files a tax return will be allocated $5,000 of TFSA Contribution room each year. This means that they can contribute up to $5,000 per year to a special registered account and any investment earnings within that account are not taxable not when they are earned or when they are withdrawn.

If you don't have the funds to contribute in 2009, the unused contribution room will be carried forward so that you can contribute $5,000 for 2009 and another $5,000 for 2010, etc. The contribution room allocation will be indexed each year (in $500 increments) based on changes to the Consumer Price Index.

Although no deduction is allowed for TFSA contributions, you can withdraw the funds at any time with no tax consequences. When you withdraw funds, new TFSA contribution room is created allowing you to put back the money without using up any contribution room allocation.

See Part One for more complete details regarding the Tax-Free Savings Account.

Maximize your RRSP contribution

Making a contribution to a deductible registered plan, like your RRSP, is a good thing if you want to claim more non-refundable credits like medical expenses on your own return or transfer certain amounts to your parents' or spouse's return. That's because net income, the figure upon which these amounts is calculated, is reduced. A low net family income will also increase federal refundable tax credits like the Child Tax Benefit, The Working Income Tax Benefit, or the GST Credits. It all means more cash for you throughout the year.

When it comes to tax advantages, investing within a registered account essentially enables some double-dipping: new dollars are created for investment purposes with your tax deduction, while tax on investment earnings is deferred into the future. That's a great game plan, and it's legal too!

But there is one catch: you will be restricted in the amounts you can sock away in your registered accounts. In the case of the RRSP, your maximum contribution is based on your "unused RRSP contribution room." If you have no available RRSP contribution room, be sure to contribute to a TFSA.

**Essential
TAX FACT #112**

The amount you can contribute to an RRSP is based on your "unused RRSP contribution room". This figure can be found on your Notice of Assessment or Reassessment.

Avoid RRSP contribution errors

Personal financial independence. That's the goal...now what's the time line? You'll achieve your dreams faster if you make it a rule to invest your maximum allowable contribution to an RRSP every year.

Unused RRSP contribution room is a notional account the CRA sets up for you when you file a tax return and report the required "earned income" for RRSP contribution purposes. Earned income is income from actively-earned sources, like employment and self-employment and will also include net rental income, CPP disability pensions and taxable alimony payments received.

Moms who work part-time, children with modelling careers, teenagers who work as babysitters or retirees who work part-time as lawn care specialists—all should file a return to build RRSP contribution room—even if they are not taxable.

By reducing net income with an RRSP deduction, family net income is decreased for the purposes of claiming refundable tax credits. That's important, because it can be lucrative. Lower net income might also enable the transfer of certain personal tax credits—like tuition, education and textbook amounts—between family members to reduce the family tax bill.

So just how much can you contribute? RRSP contribution room is the lesser of:

- 18% of earned income from the prior tax year minus any net "Pension Adjustments" (PAs) for the current year, and
- the maximum RRSP "contribution limit" for the current year minus any net Pension Adjustments for the current year.

Let's define some of those terms. The "Pension Adjustment" is a measure of benefits accruing to you as a member of another tax-deferred plan at work, such as an RPP (Registered Pension Plan) or DPSP (Deferred Profit Sharing Plan).

The RRSP "contribution limit" has been increasing of late:

2005—$16,500
2006—$18,000
2007—$19,000
2008—$20,000
2009—$21,000
2010—$22,000

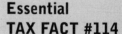
CRA provides a worksheet for calculating RRSP contribution room in its Guide: *RRSPs and Other Registered Plans for Retirement.* You might want to check this out. But usually

figuring out how much you can contribute begins with looking for your Unused Contribution Room on your Notice of Assessment or Reassessment from the CRA.

The RRSP deduction is recorded on Schedule 7 and from there on Line 208 of the tax return. This deduction can include:

- RRSP contributions made in prior years and not deducted or refunded
- RRSP contributions made in the tax year
- RRSP contributions made in the first 60 days after the end of the tax year

Age Eligibility. Note that there is no lower age limit for contributing to an RRSP. As long as CRA has the unused RRSP contribution room recorded, even a 6 year old can make a contribution. But, RRSPs must be collapsed by the end of the year in which you turn 71.

Spousal RRSPs. You may contribute to your own RRSPs based on available RRSP contribution room, and may also contribute some or all of the amounts to a spousal RRSP. This may provide for income splitting advantages on retirement and can help an age-ineligible taxpayer prolong the ability to use an RRSP deduction. Spousal RRSPs are not subject to the Attribution Rules; that is, you can contribute to a spousal RRSP and have the resulting income taxed in the spouse's hands...but there is a catch. **Withdrawals from a spousal RRSP will be taxed in the contributor's hands if the money is withdrawn within 3 years of the last contribution to any spousal plan.**

John, for example, has been making contributions every year to equalize pension accumulations. If his wife Sofi withdraws money from a spousal RRSP within three years of the last contribution by John to any spousal plan, the withdrawal will be taxed in John's hands.

An exception to this rule occurs when the spousal RRSP accumulations are transferred into a Registered Retirement Income Fund or RRIF. (See next chapter for more details in creating a pension from your RRSP accumulations). In that case only the amounts in excess of the minimum amount you are required to withdraw will be taxed in the hands of the contributor to the spousal RRSP.

If John in our example above, had turned 72 this year, he could no longer contribute to his own RRSP even though he still has unused RRSP contribution room of $5,000. His wife Sofi is 65, though. John can choose to make a spousal RRSP contribution, thereby depositing the money into Sofi's RRSP. He can then take the deduction on his return.

New pension income splitting rules may impact the amount of contributions some taxpayers make to the family's RRSP. These rules will be discussed later. But remember, double digit returns by way of tax savings will often result from an RRSP contribution; so it's good to weigh that in to every investment decision.

Essential TAX FACT #117

If you are "age ineligible" you may still contribute to a spousal RRSP, based on your RRSP contribution room, if your spouse is under 72 years old.

Essential TAX FACT #118

If you are 18 or over, an "over contribution" can be made to your RRSP—up to a maximum of $2,000.

In addition, certain "tax-free rollovers" of qualifying receipts into an RRSP will also be allowed. These will be discussed in Part Six.

The point of all of this is, of course, to increase your RRSP deduction on Line 208 of the return while deferring tax on income, reducing current taxes payable and increasing entitlements to refundable tax credits or social benefits like the Old Age Security or Employment Insurance. But, what happens if you don't need the tax deduction to reduce income? You can save the deduction for a year when you can use it!

Consider this example: Terry is an MBA student who is not taxable, but who maximizes his RRSP contribution every year. He knows that he does not need to take the tax deduction, but can save his "unused RRSP contributions" for next year, when he will be working and earning $80,000. He will get a bigger bang for his RRSP buck that way.

Essential TAX FACT #119

Any amounts contributed in the year and not deducted are considered to be "deducted RRSP contributions." These amounts may be carried forward and deducted in future years if this is advantageous.

Essential
TAX FACT #120

When RRSP contributions are made by transferring capital property into the account, you are deemed to have disposed of the property at the time of the transfer.

It can really pay off in a big way to claim your RRSP deduction when your marginal tax advantage is highest.

Consider another example: Sam is a single father with three children. He earns $45,000 at his job as a security officer and pays $6,000 per year in child care. Net income is therefore $39,000, putting him in a clawback zone for the Child Tax Benefit. This means his benefits will be reduced because he has exceeded pre-set income thresholds. If he can contribute to an RRSP he will be able to increase his Child Tax Benefit and reduce his taxes, too. Ask your tax advisor to compute your marginal tax advantages, or use your tax software to do "what if" scenarios yourself… what if I contributed $1,000, $5,000, $10,000 and so on.

But suppose you just don't have any cash to contribute to an RRSP? Here's more good news: RRSP contributions may be made in cash or in kind. That is, you may transfer an eligible investment from your non-registered invest-ments to your RRSP and may claim a deduction for the fair market value of the asset at the time of the transfer.

If the fair market value at the time of the transfer is higher than the cost of the asset, you will have to report the capital gain in income for the year.

However, here's a trap: if the fair market value of the asset is less than its cost, then the loss will be deemed to be nil. That is, it will not be claimable.

Essential
TAX FACT #121

Investments that have declined in value should not be transferred to an RRSP as the loss in value will not be deductible.

Therefore, if you want to transfer an asset which has decreased in value to your RRSP in order to create a tax deduction, it's best to sell the asset, contribute the proceeds to the RRSP and then have the RRSP repurchase the asset. This method allows you to deduct the capital loss on your tax return.

Also, be aware that any income accrued prior to the transfer of assets, such as interest, must be reported on the tax return as of the date of transfer to the RRSP.

The following are examples of qualifying investments in an RRSP:

- publicly traded shares and shares of public corporations listed on a designated exchange
- shares of small business corporations (as long as the annuitant is not a connected shareholder)
- shares of venture capital corporations
- bonds, debentures, notes, mortgages, or similar obligations of, or guaranteed by, the Government of Canada (e.g., Canada Savings Bonds) or of a province, municipality or Crown corporation
- guaranteed investment certificates issued by a Canadian trust company
- bonds, debentures, notes or similar obligations issued by a corporation listed on a designated stock exchange in or outside of Canada
- "stripped bonds"
- a mortgage, or an interest therein, in respect of real property situated in Canada
- units in a mutual fund trust
- royalty or partnership units listed on a designated stock exchange in Canada
- gold or silver bullion or certificates.

Prior to 2005, there was a limitation on the amount of foreign investments that could be held in an RRSP. These limitations have now been lifted.

Now that your have maxed your RRSP contribution advantages and your Tax-Free Savings Account contributions, let's work on your next level of tax efficient investment options: contributions to non-registered savings accounts. By maximizing your RRSP deduction, either by cash contributions or the transfer of assets you have in non-registered accounts, you should generate a sizable tax refund. Use that refund to pay off any non-deductible debt that you have or to fund contributions to a Tax-Free Savings Account for yourself and for your spouse.

Manage investment income sources

When you earn income from your investments, you can arrange your affairs within the framework of the law to:

- shelter your income from tax in the present

- defer taxation of your income into the future

- earn the types of income which attract the least amount of tax

- take advantage of our progressive tax system by splitting income with other family members

To do this, you should know when investment earnings are "realized" or reportable for tax purposes, and that not all income sources are taxed alike. To begin, there are two broad classifications of income of your investment activities noteworthy for tax purposes:

- Income from property
- Capital gains and losses

Income from property includes interest, dividends, rents and royalties. The amounts are reported on Schedule 4 of the tax return, or in the case of rental properties, a *Statement of Rental Income (Form T776).*

Capital gains and losses result from the disposition of an asset for more or less than you paid when you purchased it or its value on acquisition. Your capital transactions are reported separately on Schedule 3—*Statement of Capital Gains and Losses,* and only at the time of disposition.

Income from property vs. income from a business. Income from business and property are discussed together in the Income Tax Act and therefore are subject to many of the same general rules, when it comes to income reporting and expense deductibility.

A business is defined as a "profession, calling, trade, manufacture or under-taking of any kind whatever, and except for certain capital properties, an adventure or concern in the nature of trade." Specifically this definition does not include an office or employment, income from property or capital gains or losses. There must also be a *reasonable expectation of profit* on an annual and cumulative basis over the ownership period. That is, it must be shown that expenses have been incurred to earn gross revenues that result in a reasonable expectation of profit over time.

When you file your return, you should also know about several key restrictions on your expenses:

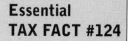

Essential TAX FACT #124

Canada's "self-assessment" system puts the onus on you, the taxpayer, to keep accurate account of revenues earned and expenses incurred to arrive at both gross and net income.

- *General limitation on expense deductibility:* No tax deduction is ever allowed except to the extent that it is reasonable in the circumstances.

- *Personal and living expenses.* No deduction is allowed for personal or living expenses unless you incur travelling expenses while away from home in carrying on business. To deal with "mixed-use expenditures" a proration is required to remove any personal component of the cost.

- *Capital outlays or loss.* Outlays, losses or replacement of capital, or a payment on account of capital other than an allowance in respect of depreciation, obsolescence or depletion of an asset used to earn rental or business income cannot be deducted. However, non-deductible capital outlays increase the tax cost of property, and will reduce any future capital gain.

- *Limitation for exempt income.* No deduction is allowed when expenses are incurred to earn exempt income, such as from a life insurance policy.

- *Limit on interest and property tax.* Interest and property taxes paid on vacant land held for resale or development are not deductible except if the land is held in the course of a business or for the primary purpose of gaining or producing income from the land.

- *Limits on RRSP contributions.* Because of its passive nature, almost all income from property is not included in the computation of "earned income" for RRSP contribution purposes. However, net income earned from a business and a rental property will qualify as RRSP earned income.

- *Reporting income from property.* Income from property is reported as received or receivable on a calendar year basis. The calendar year is also used to report income received or receivable by unincorporated businesses, although an election to use a non-calendar fiscal year may be available in the case of the active business enterprise.

- *Reporting accrued interest income.* On investment contracts acquired after 1989, interest is considered to accrue for tax purposes on the contract's anniversary date, and this accrued interest must be reported annually on the return. This is required whether or not you actually receive the interest in the year (which likely will not be the case for compounding investments.)

- *No CPP contributions on income from property.* Neither investment income or net rental income qualifies for the purposes of making CPP contributions.

Now here's the tax skinny on your investment income sources:

- **Interest Income.** This is the least efficient investment income source. The full amount of accrued income must be reported annually—so you pay tax on compounding earnings before you receive them. For this reason, taxpayers often plan to earn interest income inside registered accounts.

- **Dividends.** Dividends are the after-tax distributions of profit from a corporation. Most dividends from public corporations and certain dividends from private corporations are "grossed up" for tax purposes, so that you report 145% of the cash dividend on your return, at line 180. You can also deduct about 19% of the grossed up dividend on Schedule 1 of your return in calculating your taxes payable, and a smaller credit will also be given against provincial taxes, depending on your province of residence. As a result, such dividends are often quite tax efficient, except when they decrease your ability to claim tax credits or increase clawbacks by artificially increasing your net income.

- Most dividends from private corporations, and a few dividends from public corporations are grossed up by 25%, not 45%. The credit against federal taxes is 13⅓% of the grossed up dividend, and a provincial credit is also given. These dividends attract more tax than those described above, but do not increase net income as much, because the gross up factor is lower.

- **Rents.** It is net rental income—gross rents less operating costs and capital cost allowance—that is reported for tax purposes. Net rental earnings qualify as earned income for RRSP purposes. You can claim capital cost allowance to bring net rental income to zero, but not to create or increase a loss.

- **Royalties.** It is possible to set off some resource royalty income with a resource allowance. Starting in 2007, the resource allowance deduction will no longer be available. Resource royalties are income from property. Royalties from publishing ventures are reported as business income.

- **Capital Gains or Losses.** Although not considered to be income from property, you should know that a capital gain or loss is not "realized" for tax purposes until there is an actual or deemed disposition, and then only 50% of the gain or loss is taxable or allowable. For some capital dispositions the income inclusion rate is nil. More on this in the next chapter.

Calculate marginal tax rates on investment income

If you are going to manage your capital accumulations, you need to know your marginal tax rates on your investments. These were briefly defined in Part Two of this book.

To be completely accurate, marginal tax rates should take into account the effect of the next dollar of income on refundable tax credits and, of course, the provincial taxes. The most effective way to determine the marginal tax rate is to calculate the income taxes payable on the return, plus refundable credits, and then add $100 of the type of income that will next be earned. Note the new taxes payable plus the revised amount of refundable credits receivable. The difference is the marginal tax rate as a percentage.

**Essential
TAX FACT #125**

The marginal tax rate is the rate of tax paid on the next dollar earned or saved on the next dollar deducted. As different types of income are taxed differently, you need to understand income source, income level and rates of taxes applied to calculate your MTR.

The marginal tax rate will depend on your the type of income you earn and how much other income you have. Most types of capital gains attract one-half of the marginal tax rate for interest income, for example. The MTR for dividend income is not as easily calculated, as the dividend gross up and dividend tax credit vary with the type of dividend, and there are variations in the dividend tax credits by province. Generally, however, dividends attract a lower rate than interest, business or property income.

The MTR is an effective tool in comparing the after-tax rate of return on different investment types as well as calculating the return on investments which reduce taxable income, such as RRSP contributions.

Visit www.knowledgebureau.com/ETF for a summary of marginal tax rates on income sources.

Know the basic rules for reporting interest income

Interest income is common to most investors. It can often accrue on a compounding basis (that is, interest is reinvested rather than paid out to the investor during the term of the contract). The following are examples of debt obligations which pay interest:

- A Guaranteed Investment Certificate which features a fixed interest rate for a term spanning generally one to five years.

- A Canada Savings Bond.

- A treasury bill or zero coupon bond which provides no interest, but is sold at a discount to its maturity value.

- A strip bond or coupon.

- A Guaranteed Investment Certificate offering interest rates that rise as time goes on. These are also known as deferred interest obligations.

- An income bond or debenture where the interest paid is linked to a corporation's profit or cash flow.

- An indexed debt obligation instrument that is linked to inflation rates, such as Government of Canada Real Return Bonds.

Interest reporting follows two basic tax rules:

1. You must report the interest in the taxation year when it is actually received or receivable.

2. Compounding investments allow you to earn interest on interest during the term of the contract. In this case, you must report all interest income that accrues in the year ending on the debt's anniversary date. Although you pay tax on income you haven't received as cash, you've effectively reinvested the pre-tax interest at the same rate as the principal pays.

**Essential
TAX FACT #126**

The anniversary date of an investment contract will be either one year from its date of issue less a day, the anniversary of that date in each subsequent year, or the day of disposition. That's when accrued interest must be reported.

The issue date is important—reporting stems from that date rather than the date of ownership. Also, because of the annual reporting rules, which apply to investments acquired after 1989, an issue date in November of one year, for example, does not require interest reporting until the following year. In other words, the accrual of interest for the period November to December 31 is not required.

You should be aware that for investments acquired in the period 1981 up to and including 1989, a three year reporting cycle was required, but you could switch to annual accrual reporting if desired.

Interest income reporting is often obvious: you will receive a T5, T3 or T600 slip, depending on the investment. Interest received or accrued each year must be reported as investment income on *Schedule 4 – Statement of Investment Income*, and Line 121 of the tax return.

Essential TAX FACT #127

T Slips need not be issued for interest income under $50.

Note: you must report interest income earned even if you did not receive a T slip.

Canada Savings Bonds. Although the name implies that these debt obligations are bonds, Canada Savings Bonds do not have many of the characteristics of other bonds. They are issued by the Government of Canada, are non-marketable and redeemable on demand. After the first three months, they pay interest up to the end of the month prior to cashing; otherwise interest is paid on November 1 each year, in the case of regular bonds. Compound bonds are also available, where interest accrues but is only paid on redemption.

Essential TAX FACT #128

Many Canadians buy CSBs on a payroll deduction plan. In that case, be sure to claim the interest you pay in financing the purchase on Line 221 as a carrying charge.

Things get a little trickier when investment contracts have unique features:

- they may be non-interest bearing and sold at a discount to their maturity value
- the interest rates may be adjusted for inflation over time
- the rate of interest may increase as the term progresses
- interest payments may vary with the debtor's cash flows or profits
- where the instrument is transferred before the end of the term, a reconciliation of interest earnings must take place.

Here are some examples:

Regular government or corporate bonds can also be called "coupon bonds" and pay a stated rate of interest. If the interest is from a Canadian source it will be reported on a T5 slip and entered on the tax return in the calendar year received in the normal manner. If from a foreign source, interest is reported annually in Canadian funds on Schedule 4 and may generate a foreign tax credit if taxes have been withheld at source in the foreign country.

Zero coupon bonds, strip bonds or T-Bills (Treasury Bills) feature no stated interest rate. These are sold at a discount to their face value, and the difference between your cost and the value at maturity is interest income. You will need to report the interest accrued each year on the anniversary date.

Further complications arise when the bond or coupon is sold before maturity. In that case, the new investor receives interest on the next payment date, as usual, even though some of the interest may have accrued prior to the purchase. An adjustment must be made to ensure each bond owner reports the correct amount of interest up to the date ownership change. In addition, a capital gain or loss might arise on the disposition.

Understand tax consequences of asset dispositions

To understand the tax consequences on disposition of an income-producing asset, a short lesson in capital gains or losses is required. We will be discussing capital acquisitions and dispositions in more depth in the next chapter on Wealth Preservation, but by way of introduction, you should know the following basic terms.

In a mathematical equation, a capital gain (or loss) looks like this:

Capital Gain (or Loss) = **Proceeds of Disposition**
minus Adjusted Cost Base
minus Outlays and Expenses Incurred

The *proceeds of disposition* will normally be the actual sales price received. But proceeds can also be a "deemed" amount (the fair market value, for example) in cases where there is a taxable disposition but no money changes hands—on death, or gifting or emigration, for example.

The *adjusted cost base* starts with the cost of an income-producing asset when acquired. This could be the cash outlay, or in the case of acquisition by way of a transfer by gift, inheritance, etc., the fair market value at the time of transfer. The ACB may also be increased or decreased by certain adjustments: the cost of improvements to the asset, for example, or in the case of land, non-deductible interest or property taxes.

For example, Jonas buys shares for $100 plus $10 commission and sells them six months later for $200 less $20 commission.

- The "Adjusted Cost Base" of the shares is $110 (price paid, including commissions).
- The "Proceeds of Disposition" are $200.
- The $20 commission on sale is an "outlay and expense" of sale.
- The "Capital Gain" is $200 - $110 - $20 = **$70.**

Report interest from T-Bills and bonds properly

How do you report income when there is an interest component and you later sell the asset for more than its cost base? Some illustrations follow:

Treasury Bills. These are short-term government debt obligations, generally available in three, six or twelve month terms. If the T-Bill's term exceeds one year, the normal annual interest accrual rules would apply.

T-Bills are similar to strip bonds (discussed below) because they are acquired at a discount to their maturity value and have no stated interest rate. On maturity you will usually receive their face value, which will include the accrued interest amount. This is generally reported on a T5008 slip. If you sell the T-Bill before maturity, a capital gain or loss could result. This is how you would calculate the tax consequences:

1. Calculate the interest that has accrued in the period of ownership. Report this as interest income on the tax return.

2. Calculate the proceeds of disposition less the interest accrued.

3. Reduce this figure by the adjusted cost base.

4. Subtract any outlays and expenses, such as brokerage fees.

5. The result is the capital gain or loss.

For example, a T-Bill with a face value of $10,000 is acquired for $9,600 and a brokerage fee of $50. The T-bill matures 365 days after it was acquired. The bill was disposed of before end of term for $9,900, and a brokerage fee of $40 was paid. It had been held for 188 days.

1. Interest to be reported = $10,000 − $9,600 = $400 x 188/365 = $206.03. The brokerage fee of $50 is claimed as a carrying charge on Line 221.

2. Calculate Adjusted Cost Base: $9,600 + $206.03 = $9,806.03.

3. Capital Gain on Disposition: $53.97, calculated as follows: Proceeds of Disposition = $9,900 less ACB $9,806.03 less Outlays and Expenses $40 = **$53.97**.

Strip Bonds. These are also known as zero-coupon bonds as they do not pay interest during the period of ownership. They are purchased at a discount and if held to term will yield a future value that is higher. The difference between the present and future value is considered to be the interest paid over the period to maturity. The resulting interest must be reported annually on the anniversary date of the bond's issue date each year.

Here's an example:

The yield on a 5 year bond sold at a discount of 20% of the face value is 4.564% $[(10,000/8,000)^{(1/5)} - 1]$ so the interest accrued on the bond would be:

Year	Interest	Value
0		$ 8,000.00
1	$ 365.12	$ 8,365.12
2	$ 381.78	$ 8,746.90
3	$ 399.20	$ 9,146.10
4	$ 417.42	$ 9,563.52
5	$ 436.48	$10,000.00

If the bond sold for $9,000 with three years remaining, the yield to maturity would be 3.5744% [(10,000/9,000)$^{(1/3)}$ – 1] so the interest accrued after the sale to the new owner would be:

Year	Interest	Value
0		$ 9,000.00
1	$ 321.70	$ 9,321.70
2	$ 333.19	$ 9,654.89
3	$ 345.11	$10,000.00

On disposition before maturity, accrued interest is added in calculating the adjusted cost base, outlays and expenses are deducted to compute the capital gain or loss. The adjusted cost base for the new owner is the cost of the property ($9,000 in this case).

Indexed Debt Obligations include, in addition to interest paid on the amount invested, a payment (or deduction) on maturity that represents the decrease (or increase) in the purchasing power of the investment during the term of the investment. This additional payment is reported according to the normal annual accrual rules. If in the year of disposition or maturity it is determined that interest has been over-accrued the overaccrual can be deducted as a carrying charge on Schedule 4.

Income Bonds and Income Debentures. A special type of bond or debenture may be issued with a term of up to 5 years by corporations that are in financial difficulty and under the control of a receiver or trustee in bankruptcy. A return on such an income bond is paid only if the issuing corporation earns a profit from its operations. Such amounts paid or received by the investor are then treated as a dividend for tax purposes.

Exchanges of Debentures for Securities. When a bond or debenture is exchanged for shares of a corporation, the exchange is not considered to be a disposition for tax purposes, providing that the share is received directly from the corporation which issued it. Therefore there are no tax consequences. This is also true when one debenture is exchanged for another bond or debenture, providing that the principal amount is the same.

Maximize tax opportunities with dividends

A return of the after-tax profits of a corporation to its shareholders is known as a "dividend". Dividends received from Canadian corporations are subject to special rules, as an adjustment must be made to compensate for the taxes already paid by the corporation.

The adjustment varies depending on the rate of tax the corporation paid on the income from which dividend is paid.

If the dividend is paid from income that attracted a high rate of corporate tax, the dividend is called an 'eligible dividend' and is grossed up by 45%. Public corporations almost invariably issue eligible dividends. The grossed up dividend is reported directly at line 120.

If the dividend is paid from income that attracted a low rate of tax (generally within a private corporation), the dividend is grossed up by 25% and reported at line 180. Dividends reported at line 180 are included in total dividends reported at line 120.

The grossed up dividend generates a Dividend Tax Credit, both federally and provincially. These credits reduce taxes otherwise payable. If the dividend is eligible, the federal dividend tax credit is 18.9655% of the grossed up dividend. If the dividend is not eligible, the dividend tax credit is 13⅓% of the grossed up dividend. The federal dividend tax credit is claimed on Schedule 1.

Provincial dividend tax credits vary by province, and are calculated on the related provincial tax calculation form.

Because the dividend "gross up" artificially increases net income, it may reduce your refundable or non-refundable tax credits, such as:

- The Canada Child Tax Benefit
- The GST Credit
- The Working Income Tax Benefit
- Provincial refundable tax credits
- The Age Amount
- The Spousal Amount
- Amount for Eligible Dependant

- Medical expenses
- Amounts for Other Adult Dependants.

It may also negatively affect other financial transactions that are dependent upon the size of net income on the tax return:

- Old Age Security Clawbacks
- Employment Insurance Clawbacks
- Guaranteed Income Supplements
- Provincial per diem rates for nursing homes
- Certain provincial medical/prescription plans.

Obviously, eligible dividends have a greater impact on your ability to claim these credits or to avoid clawback, as they are grossed up by 45%. On the other hand, the dividend tax credit for such dividends is also greater than it is for non-eligible dividends.

If your income is high enough that you are not eligible for these tax credits and you are already fully clawed back, eligible dividends attract a fairly low rate of tax. If you can claim the credits or are subject to clawback, eligible dividends will attract a fairly high overall MTR. On the other hand, the MTR on eligible dividends for lower income taxpayers is often negative (because the dividend tax credit exceeds the taxes owing on the dividend income).

Therefore income planning around investment options is important, especially for seniors, and should take into account all these rules.

You should be aware of the tax consequences of the following types of dividends:

- *Capital Dividends.* Sometimes a shareholder in a private corporation may receive a Capital Dividend. Such dividends are not taxable.

  To qualify as a Capital Dividend, the dividend must be paid out of the Capital Dividend Account (CDA) of a private Canadian corporation. This account is set up to accumulate the non-taxable (50%) portion of any capital gains realized by the corporation, capital dividends

> **Essential**
> **TAX FACT #132**
>
> A taxpayer can earn over a significant amount of eligible dividends on a tax free basis, depending on the province of residence. This is an example of a tax-efficient income source for some taxpayers.

received from other corporations, untaxed portions of gains realized on the disposition of eligible capital property, and life insurance proceeds received by the corporation.

- *Capital Gains Dividends.* These are dividends received from a mutual fund company. They are reported on a T5 Slip and Schedule 3. Capital gains dividends are considered to be capital gains and not dividends (that is, they are taxed at 50%, are not grossed up and are not eligible for the dividend tax credit).

- *Stock Dividends.* This type of dividend arises when a corporation decides to issue additional shares to its existing shareholders, instead of paying a cash dividend. Like regular dividends, stock dividends must be included in income, and are subject to gross-up, and the dividend tax credit. The amount of the dividend is the amount that the corporation adds to its capital accounts on issuing the share. Where the stock dividend is paid by a public company, this is usually the fair market value of the share.

The corporation will issue a T5 slip to the recipient of a dividend in almost all cases.

Income Splitting Opportunities. A special rule allows the transfer of dividends from one spouse to another if by doing so a Spousal Amount is created or increased. The dividend income is left off the lower-income spouse's tax return and is reported by the higher-income spouse, who can then use the offsetting dividend tax credit. See more on income splitting at the end of this chapter.

**Essential
TAX FACT #133**

When it comes to your mutual funds, income realized along the way can affect your eventual gain or loss when you sell the units. This is an essential tax fact that can really save you money in the future.

Manage mutual fund, income trust and segregated fund transactions with savvy

Many people buy units in mutual fund trusts, yet few people really understand the tax consequences and the requirement to keep track of the adjusted cost base of their investment.

The term "adjusted cost base" came up earlier in the discussion of bond dispositions. There you could see that this is a critical figure in computing your gains or losses when an investment is disposed of.

When you buy a mutual fund, it is important to record the cost and number of units acquired for use in calculating the Adjusted Cost Base. Start a spread sheet and record each investment's cost, including commissions and the number of units acquired. The total adjusted cost base is divided by the number of units to arrive at the cost per unit.

Example: Units acquired: 1,000. Adjusted Cost Base: $10,000. Per unit: $10.00

Tax treatment of distributions. Your adjusted cost base and unit costs will likely be adjusted during the holding period of your investment as mutual funds are required to distribute all interest, dividends, other income and net capital gains to their unit holders at least once every year. With the exception of any return of capital, these distributions are taxable. In the year you acquire a mutual fund, you will usually receive a full annual distribution, even if you invested late in the year.

A T3 Slip (from a mutual fund trust) or a T5 Slip (from a mutual fund corporation) will report these distributions in the proper income categories. Rarely is this income received in cash. Rather, it is used to buy more units in the fund and those reinvested amounts are added to the Adjusted Cost Base. Accounting for such increases in the ACB will ensure that you report the minimum capital gain (or maximum capital loss) when you sell the units in the future.

Example: The mutual fund in the above example paid $1,000 in income distributions in Year 2. The money was reinvested and now the taxpayer has 1,080 units.

Units held: 1,080 Adjusted Cost Base: $11,000 Per unit $10.19

Switches and exchanges. In general, when you exchange an investment in one fund for another (e.g. from an equity fund to a balanced fund), a taxable disposition is considered to have occurred, with normal tax consequences—if your investment is in a mutual fund trust. There are no tax consequences when you switch from one class or series to another class or series of funds—if the investment is in corporate class funds.

Tax consequences upon disposition of the units. When you sell or otherwise dispose of a mutual fund, a taxable capital gain or loss may result. Mutual fund units or shares are classified as "identical properties" for tax purposes. The average cost of the shares/units must be calculated each time there is a purchase or sale, by dividing total units owned into the adjusted cost of the units/shares including all reinvested earnings, as illustrated above. This provides you with the cost per unit required to calculate the capital gains or losses properly. Please see the next chapter for more information on computing capital gains or losses; however, in the meantime, use the column headings shown on your spreadsheet to track the numbers properly.

Date	Cost plus commission	Plus reinvested distributions	Less return of capital	Less ACB of units redeemed	Total	Divided by no. of units	ACB per unit

Income Trusts. Income trusts are trust entities set up in recent years to manage the affairs of a business and flow the profits of the business to the investors (or unit holders) directly rather than having the business pay corporate taxes and then pass the remaining profits to the shareholders as dividends. Since corporate taxes are avoided, the income from the income trust exceeds the dividends that could be paid by the corporation if corporate income taxes were paid. The income from income trusts then is ordinary investment income and not dividends. The income is reported to the investor on a T3 slip and reported on Schedule 4 with no gross up and no dividend tax credit is available. For most income trusts, these rules will be changing beginning in 2011 when the trust will be required to pay the equivalent of corporate income taxes on the income before flowing it through to the unit holders. In some cases, income trusts may pay a return of capital to the unit holders. As with mutual funds, the return of capital portion of the income is not taxable, but will reduce the adjusted cost base of the trust units and therefore increase any capital gain on their disposition.

Segregated Funds. A segregated fund is similar to a mutual fund in that it is a pooled investment. However it is established by an insurance company and the funds invested are segregated from the rest of the capital of the company. The main difference between a segregated and a mutual fund is in the guarantee—that a minimum amount will always be returned to the investor regardless of the performance of the fund over time.

Essential TAX FACT #134

Within a segregated fund, the policyholder does not own the units; the segregated fund trust does. Therefore income allocations do not affect the value of the fund.

Income that is allocated out to segregated fund unit holders is reported on a T3 Slip, as the insurance company will have set up a trust for the purposes of creating the segregated fund. Dividend income received from the fund will be eligible for the dividend tax credit, interest will be taxed in the normal manner and any foreign taxes paid on foreign income allocations will qualify for the foreign tax credit.

There are many differences between a mutual fund trust and a segregated fund trust.

When income—interest, dividends or capital gains or losses—is distributed as a result of investment performance, it will be received in the hands of the trust, which then allocates the income out on the basis of units to the investors. Unlike a regular mutual fund, a segregated fund can allocate a loss to the unitholder.

Such income allocations do not affect the value of the segregated fund. This is not the case when you receive distributions out of a mutual fund, as these will affect the value of the mutual fund (it will generally go down on the day of distribution).

Another important investment and tax planning feature of segregated funds is that allocations made from such a fund can take into account the length of time the investor has owned the units. When a mutual fund distributes income, all unit holders receive a share of the distributions as of the day of the distribution, even if they have only held the funds for one day. This can generate a large and unwanted tax liability if the unit holder is not aware.

Segregated funds also offer maturity and death guarantees on the capital invested and specifically, reset guarantees—which is the ability to lock in market gains. This can be from 75% to 100% of the amount invested, which will be returned to the taxpayer on death or maturity.

Depending on the insurer, a reset can be initiated by the investor two to four times per year. The guaranteed period on maturity is usually 10 years after the policy is purchased, or after the reset. There are no tax consequences at the time the accrued gains in the investment are locked in by way of reset. This can be a very attractive feature of this investment type.

Guarantee at maturity. If at maturity the value of the fund has dropped, the insurer must top up the fund by contributing additional assets to bring the value up to the guaranteed amount. There are no tax implications at the time of top up. However, there will be when the taxpayer disposes of the fund. This will be the difference between the ACB (which includes allocations of income over time) and the proceeds received.

Guarantee at death. The policyholder is deemed to have disposed of the contract at its fair market value at time of deemed disposition—death or emigration for example. If the value of the assets in the fund increases, the gain will be taxable to the policyholder when the policy matures or to his estate if the policy owner dies. If the value of the assets in the fund decreases, the taxpayer is deemed to have acquired additional notional units in the fund so that no gain is incurred even though the taxpayer receives more than the value of the notional units. A capital loss may occur if the guaranteed value is less than 100% of the investment.

Know tax rules behind your revenue properties

Many have invested in real property to get a lift out of their investment dollar. If that investment is in a principal residence, a tax free gain on the sale of your home is possible. This is so even if you earn income from that tax exempt residence—by renting out a room or rooms, for example, or by running a business from your home. We'll dig deeper into the tax consequences of primary and secondary residences or rental properties in the next chapter, but our mandate here is to discuss revenue properties held for investment purposes.

**Essential
TAX FACT #135**

One tax exempt principal residence can be owned per household.

Those who collect rental income from a property rented to tenants will have tax consequences in operating the property and usually upon the disposition of the property as well.

In the first year, it is important to set up the tax reporting for a revenue property properly:

- *A Statement of Rental Income (Form T776)* must be completed.

- Income and expenses will be reported on a calendar year basis. Technically, a landlord is supposed to use accrual accounting in reporting revenues and expenses. As a practical matter, there are generally few major differences between cash and accrual accounting for individual landlords, and most individuals report rental income on a cash basis. The CRA will accept cash accounting so long as the cash income does not differ significantly from accrual income.

- Gross rental income must be reported. It is best to open a separate bank account to keep this in. If you rent to someone you are related to, you must account for fair market value rents if you rent for less.

- Advance payments of rent can be included in income according to the years they relate to.

- Lease cancellation payments received are included in rental income.

- In order to deduct operating expenses from rental income, there must be a reasonable expectation of profit on an annual basis.

- Fully deductible operating expenses include maintenance, repairs, supplies, interest, taxes.

- Partially deductible expenses could include the business portion of auto expenses and meal and entertainment expenses incurred.

- Expenditures for asset acquisition or improvement cannot be deducted in full. Rather Capital Cost Allowance (CCA) schedules must be set up to account for depreciation expense.

- As land is not a depreciable asset, it is necessary to separate the cost of land and buildings on the CCA schedule.

- CCA is always taken at your option. It is possible to forego making any claim at all in one year to preserve it for the future. A rental loss cannot be created or increased with a CCA claim. CCA classes and rates are discussed in more detail in Part Six.

- Not deductible are any expenses that relate to personal living expenses of the owner, or any expenses that relate to the cost of the land or principal portions of loans taken to acquire or maintain the property.

When you rent a portion of your home to a family member for a nominal rent you may not claim a rental loss, as there is no reasonable expectation of profit. In this case, you need not include the rent in income.

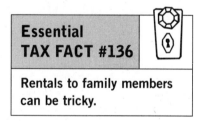

Essential TAX FACT #136

Rentals to family members can be tricky.

As noted above, expenses are usually deducted on a cash basis as paid, so long as this does not result in a material difference from accrual basis accounting. If you account on an accrual basis, expenses are to be matched with the revenue to which they relate, so that expenses prepaid in one year are not deducted then but in the later year to which they relate.

Deductible Expenses. Common deductible operating expenses include:

Advertising—Amounts paid to advertise the availability of the rental property

Essential
TAX FACT #137

If an expenditure extends the useful life of the property or improves upon the original condition of the property, then the expenditure is capital in nature.

Essential
TAX FACT #138

A deduction for Capital Cost Allowance cannot increase or create a rental loss. In the case of multiple property ownership, this rule is applied to the net profits of all properties together.

Capital Cost Allowance—Special and important rules apply regarding restorations improvements:

Improvements that extend the useful life of the property (new roof, new fence or new carpeting for example) must be listed on the Capital Cost Allowance schedule, resulting in only a portion of the expenditure being currently deductible under the CCA rules. On the other hand, a *repair* that returns the property to its original state, such as replacing a piece of the carpet, is a current expense, which is 100% deductible.

Condominium fees applicable to the period when the rental condo was available for rent may be deducted.

Insurance—If the insurance is prepaid for future years, claim only the portion that applies to the rental year, unless you are using cash basis accounting.

Landscaping costs may be deducted in the year paid.

Lease cancellation payments by landlord—Deduct that portion of the payment made as landlord to the person who leased the property according to the amount that relates to the period of the cancelled lease in each year. That is, the landlord will need to deduct these amounts over the term of the lease including renewal periods. In the case of dispositions at arm's length, a final amount may be deducted, but based on the current capital gains inclusion rate (50%). The full amount of the lease cancellation payment may be deducted on a sale if the building was considered to be inventory rather than capital property.

Legal, accounting and other professional fees—There are unique rules to consider in deducting fees paid to professionals:

- Legal fees to prepare leases or to collect rent are deductible.
- Legal fees to acquire the property form part of the cost of the property.

- Legal fees on the sale of the property are outlays and expenses which will reduce any capital gain on the sale.

- Accounting fees to prepare statements, keep books, or prepare the tax return are deductible.

Maintenance and repairs—Costs of regular maintenance and minor repairs are deductible. For major repairs, it must be determined if the cost is a current expense or capital in nature.

Management and administration fees—If you pay a third party to manage or otherwise look after some aspect of the property, the amount paid is deductible. Note that if a caretaker is given a suite in an apartment block as compensation for caretaking, a T4 Slip must be issued to report the fair market value of the rent as employment income.

Mortgage interest—Interest on a mortgage to purchase the property plus any interest on additional loans to improve the rental property may be deducted, provided you can show there is a reasonable expectation of profit from the revenue property. Note:

- If an additional mortgage is taken out against the equity in the property and the proceeds are used for some other purpose, the mortgage interest is not deductible as a rental expense, but may be deductible as a carrying charge if the proceeds were used to earn investment income.

- Other charges relating to the acquisition of a mortgage (banking fees, for example) are not deductible in the year paid, but can be amortized over a five-year period starting at the time they were incurred.

- If the interest costs relate to the acquisition of depreciable property, you may elect to add the interest to the capital cost of the asset rather than deduct it in the year paid. This will be beneficial if, for example, the property generates a rental loss and you cannot use that loss to reduce your taxes owing.

Motor vehicle expenses—Travelling expenses are generally considered to be personal living expenses of the landlord. If you own only one rental property, then motor vehicle expenses to collect rent are not deductible. However, if you personally travel to make repairs to the

Essential TAX FACT #139

If you own rental properties at two or more sites away from your place of residence, CRA will allow motor vehicle costs to collect rent, supervise repairs or otherwise manage the properties.

property, then the cost of transporting tools and materials to the property may be deducted.

Office and office supplies—Office and other supplies used up in earning rental income are deductible as are home office expenses in situations where you use the office to keep books or serve tenants.

Property taxes—These are deductible.

Renovations for the disabled—Costs incurred to make the rental property accessible to individuals with a mobility impairment may be fully deducted.

Travel costs—The same rules apply here as for motor vehicle costs. Also travel costs to supervise a revenue property do no include the cost of accommodation, which CRA considers to be a personal expense.

Utilities—If costs are paid by the landlord and not reimbursed by the tenant, they will be deductible. Costs charged to tenants are deductible if amounts collected are included in rental income.

Multiple Owners. When two or more taxpayers jointly own a revenue property, it is necessary to determine whether they own the property as co-owners or as partners in a partnership. If a partnership exists, CCA is claimed before the partnership income is allocated to the partners. In effect, all the partners are subject to the same CCA claim. If a co-ownership exists, each owner can claim CCA individually on their share of the capital costs.

Part Six covers the consequences of revenue property dispositions.

**Essential
TAX FACT #140**

If you gift or transfer money or assets to your spouse or minor children, the income is usually "attributed back" to you (transferor) and added to your income.

Avoid Attribution Rules on family income splitting

Canadians are taxed as individuals, not as economic units or households. Because of the advantages of income splitting under our progressive tax system with its graduated tax rates—that is, the more you earn the higher your rate of tax—we are generally prohibited from obtaining a tax advantage by splitting income with family members.

The details are set out in the Attribution Rules. Specifically, the Income Tax Act covers these rules as follows:

Transfers and loans to spouse or common-law partner. If you transfer or loan property either directly or indirectly, by means of a trust or any other means to a spouse or common-law partner for that person's benefit, any resulting income or loss or capital gain or loss from that property is taxable to you.

Transfers and loans to minors. Where property is transferred or loaned either directly or indirectly to a person who is under 18 and who does not deal with you at arm's length or who is your niece or nephew, the income or loss resulting from such property is reported by you until the transferee attains 18 years of age. Capital gains or losses do not, however, attribute back to you.

These rules thwart an otherwise perfect investment opportunity: the transfer of assets from the higher earner to the lower earners in the family to take advantage of their lower tax brackets, leading to lower total tax payable, and more after-tax funds for the family!

However, where there are rules, there are exceptions, which is true of the Attribution Rules as well. But, let's cover off the tax filing basics on income splitting first:

Facts on Asset Transfers to the Spouse

- Assets transferred to a spouse will result in the income and capital gains resulting from investment of those assets being taxed in the transferor's hands.

- Where a spouse guarantees the repayment of a loan to a spouse, made for investment purposes, attribution will apply to any income earned from the loaned funds.

Facts on Asset Transfers to a Minor Child

- Income resulting from assets transferred to a minor child will trigger attribution of rental, dividend or interest income, but not capital gains.

There are certain exceptions to the Attribution Rules:

- *Tax-Free Savings Accounts.* If you make contributions to a Tax-Free Savings Account for your spouse or children they will earn income on those deposits with no income tax payable, either by them or by you, so long as the contribution is a true gift and not a scheme to allow you to earn that income on a tax-free basis. If your spouse has no other taxable income, these earnings will have no effect on your ability to claim the spousal amount.

- *Spousal RRSPs.* Attribution does not apply to contributions made to a spousal RRSP, unless there is a withdrawal within three years. This is discussed in greater detail above.

- *Wages paid to spouse and children.* Where a spouse or children receive a wage from the family business, the attribution rules won't apply if the wage is reasonable, and is included in the recipient's income.

- *Interest income from Child Tax Benefit (CTB) or Universal Child Care Benefit (UCCB) payments.* If CTB or UCCB payments are invested in the name of a child, the income will not be subject to attribution. In other words, interest, dividends and other investment income may be reported in the hands of the child. Be sure this account remains untainted by birthday money and other gifts.

**Essential
TAX FACT #141**

The Attribution Rules will apply to joint accounts held by parents and minor children as well as spouses.

- *Joint accounts.* T5 Slips are issued by banks in the names of the account holders to report earnings on investments including interest and dividends. This does not mean that the income on those slips is taxable to those whose names are on the slips. Instead, report income on the return of the individuals who contributed the funds to the account in the proportion that the funds were supplied. For example, if only one spouse in a family works and is the source of all of the deposits, then all of the interest earned on the account is taxable to that person, no matter whose name is on the account.

- *Transfers for fair market consideration.* The Attribution Rules will not apply to any income, gain or loss from transferred property if, at the time of transfer, consideration was paid for the equivalent of fair market value for the transferred property by the transferee. The person acquiring the property must use his or her own capital to pay for it.

- *Transfers for indebtedness.* The Attribution Rules on investment income will not apply if the lower income spouse borrowed capital from higher earner, and the parties signed a bona fide loan that bore an interest rate equal to the *lesser* of:
  - the "prescribed" interest rates in effect at the time the indebtedness was incurred and
  - the rate that would have been charged by a commercial lender.

- *Payment of interest on inter-spousal loans.* Interest must actually be paid on the indebtedness incurred by the spouse, under a formal loan agreement described above, by January 30 of each year, following the tax year, or attribution will apply to income earned with the loaned funds.

- *Transfer to a spouse.* A special rule applies when property is transferred to a spouse. Normally, such property transfers at tax cost, so that no gain or loss arises. This is true even if the spouse pays fair value for the property. The property will not transfer at tax cost, but at fair market value, provided the transferor files an election to have this happen with the tax return for the year of transfer. Unless this election is made, the attribution rules will apply to the property, even if the spouse has paid fair value consideration.

- *Assets transferred to an adult child (over 18).* This will in general not be subject to attribution. However, when income splitting is the main reason for the loan to an adult child, the income will be attributed back to the transferor. An exception again occurs when a bona fide loan is drawn up with interest payable as described above, by January 30 of the year following the end of the calendar year.

- *When spouses live apart.* If spouses are living separate and apart due to relationship breakdown, they can jointly elect to have Attribution Rules not apply to the period in which they were living apart. The Attribution Rules do not apply after a divorce is finalized.

- *The kiddie tax.* The Attribution Rules will not apply when an amount is included in the calculation of Tax on Split Income on Line 424 on Schedule 1 of the tax return. This special tax is assessed on income earned by minor children from their parents' or other relatives' ventures. Specifically, dividends or shareholder benefits earned either directly or through a trust or partnership, from a corporation controlled by someone related to the child, are extracted from the normal tax calculations and reported on *Form T1206* so that tax on this income can be calculated at the highest marginal rates.

- *Assignment of Canada Pension Plan benefits.* It is possible to apply to split CPP benefits between spouses, thereby minimizing tax on that income source in some cases.

- *Pension income splitting.* The election to split pension income between spouses does not involve the actual transfer of funds from one spouse to another but an election to have the split pension taxed as if it were the other spouse's income. As such, the attribution rules do not apply. (However, if funds are actually transferred from one spouse to the other, the attribution rules will apply).

- *Investments in spouse's business.* Investments in the spouse's or common-law partner's business venture are not subject to Attribution Rules as the resulting income is business income rather than income from property.

- *Second generation earnings.* Where the income earned on property transferred to the spouse must be reported by the transferor, any secondary income earned on investing such income is taxed in the hands of the transferee.

- *Spousal dividend transfers.* One spouse may report dividends received from taxable Canadian corporations received by the other spouse if by doing so a Spousal Amount is created or increased.

- *Inheritances.* Attribution does not apply to inheritances.

- *Additional attribution avoidance strategies:*
  - Have the higher income spouse pay household and personal expenses, and the lower income spouse acquire investment assets with income earned in his or her own right.
  - Reinvest spouse's income tax refunds and refundable tax credits.
  - Contribute to an RESP for your child. Accumulate education savings on a tax-deferred basis, as discussed below.

Maximize tax preferred education savings

Essential TAX FACT #143

There is a further tax incentive for educational savings under the RESP: the Canada Education Savings Grant.

An RESP is a tax-assisted savings plan set up for the purposes of funding a beneficiary's future education costs. It also serves as a way to split income earned in the plan with the beneficiary, who will be taxed at a lower rate than the contributor, as a general rule, when earnings are withdrawn.

A contributor can invest up to $50,000 per beneficiary as a lifetime maximum. Annual contribution limits in place prior to 2007 are no longer in effect.

The following rules apply to RESPs:

- The plan must terminate after 35 years (unless the beneficiary is disabled).
- Minor siblings can substitute as plan beneficiaries if the intended beneficiary does not become a qualifying recipient.

Transfers may be made between RESPs with no income tax consequences.

The subscriber, who contributes money into the plan, does not receive a tax deduction at the time of investment. However, income earned within the plan on the contributions is tax-deferred until the beneficiary student qualifies to receive education assistance from the plan by starting to attend post-secondary school, either on a part-time or on a full-time basis.

The Canada Education Savings Grant provides additional funds for education. This grant is added to the RESP each year by the Department of Human Resources and Skills Development. The grant is received on a tax-free basis by the plan. Started in 1998, it provides for a federal grant of 20% of the first $2,500 contributed to an RESP for children under the age of 18. The lifetime maximum CESG is $7,200.

To receive the money, the beneficiary of the RESP must have a Social Insurance Number. The CESG room of up to $500 a year (20% of $2,500) can be maximized each year including the year the child turns 17. Unused CESG contribution room can be carried forward until the child turns 18, however, the grant may not exceed $1,000 a year. This means that the catch-up of the grants is limited to two years at a time.

The Canada Learning Bond. The first time a child becomes eligible to receive benefits under the National Child Benefit, which is part of the Child Tax Benefit calculations, an initial Canada Learning Bond entitlement of $500 is available. This will generally happen under one of two circumstances:

- the year of birth or
- a subsequent year if the family net income is too high in the year of birth.

**Essential
TAX FACT #144**

A Canada Learning Bond increases RESP savings for lower income families.

The entitlement is $100 in each subsequent year that the family qualifies for the NCB until the year the child turns 15. Once 16, the CLB is no longer allocated to the child.

In order to turn the entitlement into real money, the Canada Learning Bond must be transferred into a Registered Education Saving Plan (RESP) for the benefit of the child. This can be done at any time before the child turns 21. If the CLB is not transferred to an RESP by the time the child turns 21, the entitlement will be lost.

The Canada Learning Bond transfers to an RESP do not otherwise affect the limits of contributions to the RESP. CLB amounts are not eligible for the Canada Education Savings Grant.

No interest is paid on unclaimed Canada Learning Bonds so it is important that the CLB be transferred to an RESP as quickly as possible so that the amount can begin to earn income.

In the year the child is born, if the parents are eligible for the National Child Benefit Supplement, the parents should:

- obtain a social insurance number for the child (required for an RESP)
- open an RESP account with the new child as beneficiary
- apply to have the Canada Learning Bond amount transferred to the new RESP.

Education Assistance Payments. When a student is ready to go to post-secondary school full time, payments can be made out of an RESP. These are called Education Assistance Payments (EAPs). The amounts represent earnings in the plan and are taxable to the student on Line 130 of the return. Contributions may be returned to the subscriber or paid to the student with no income tax consequences.

For full-time studies, the maximum EAP is $5,000 until the student has completed 13 consecutive weeks in a qualifying education program at a post-secondary educational institution. Once the 13-weeks have been completed, there is no limit to the amount that may be withdrawn from the plan. For part-time students, who spend a minimum of 12 hours a month on course-work, the maximum EAP is $2,500 per 13-week semester. Beneficiaries under an RESP are allowed to receive EAP's for up to six months after ceasing enrolment in a qualifying educational program. However, if, for a period of 12 months, the student does not enroll in a qualifying education program, the 13-week period and the $5,000 limitation will be imposed again.

If the student does not attend post-secondary school by the time s/he reaches the age of 31, and there are no qualifying substitute beneficiaries, the contributions can go back to the original subscriber. If this happens, the income earned in the plan over the years will become taxable to the subscriber, and the income is subject to a special penalty tax of 20% in addition to the regular taxes payable. Such income inclusions are called "Accumulated Income Payments" or AIPs. *Form T1172* must be completed to compute this tax.

As an alternative, if the subscriber has unused RRSP contribution room, AIPs can be transferred into the subscriber's RRSP, up to a lifetime maximum of $50,000. If amounts are transferred to an RRSP, *Form T1171* may be used to reduce or eliminate tax withheld on the AIP.

Note, the CESG will form part of the EAPs. If amounts are withdrawn from the RESP for purposes other than EAP payments, the lesser of the undistributed CESG amounts and 20% of the amount withdrawn will be returned to the Department of Human Resources by the RESP. Should the beneficiary be required to repay any CESG amounts received as Educational Assistance Payments, a deduction for the amount repaid may be taken.

You may want to consider using a Tax-Free Savings Account as an adjunct to an RESP for accumulating funds for your child's education. Although the TFSA does not have the added incentives of the CESG or CESB, it does offer flexibility that is not available in the RESP. There are no time limits on the contributions, no age limits on the beneficiaries, and no limits to the amount that can be withdrawn in any given year, and the withdrawals will not have to be reported in income—whether the beneficiary becomes a student or not.

Maximize savings for the disabled

An Registered Disability Savings Plan is a tax-assisted savings plan set up to provide financial assistance to a disabled beneficiary. While the plan does not offer a tax deduction to the contributor, the government provides generous additional contributions as well as tax-deferred earnings within the plan. See Part One for details of the contribution limits, the contribution matching through the Canada Disability Savings Grant, and the assistance for low-income taxpayers through the Canada Disability Savings Bond.

Deduct professional fees, interest and carrying charges

When you incur expenses to invest your money, a tax deduction is allowed but only if the expenses are incurred to earn income outside of registered accounts. Known as "carrying charges," eligible expenses are all reported on *Schedule 4—Statement of Investment Income*. The total carrying charges are then deducted on Line 221 and serve to offset other income of the year, so they can be lucrative. Examples of deductible carrying charges include:

- The safety deposit box.

- Accounting fees relating to the preparation of tax schedules for investment income reporting.

- Investment counsel fees. These do not include commissions paid on buying or selling investments. These commissions form part of the Adjusted Cost Base of the investment, or reduce proceeds of disposition from the investment.

- Taxable benefits reported on the T4 Slip for employer-provided loans that were used for investment purposes.

- Canada Savings Bonds payroll deduction charge.

- Life insurance policy interest costs if an investment loan was taken against cash values.

- Management or safe custody fees.

- Foreign non-business taxes not claimed as a federal or provincial foreign tax credit.

- Interest paid on investment loans if there is a reasonable expectation of income from the investment, even if the value of the investment has diminished.

- Brokerage fees* paid to secure debt obligations such as strip bonds may be claimed as a deduction. In addition, brokerage fees paid for investment counsel are deductible as a carrying charge. To be deductible, these investment counsel fees must be specific to buying and selling specific securities or to manage those securities. If they are charged by a stockbroker who also may be charging a commission for the trades themselves, the investment counsel fees must be separately billed.

*Note that if brokerage fees are paid to buy shares or other securities, they are treated as part of the Adjusted Cost Base (ACB) of the securities and reported on *Schedule 3 Capital Gains and Losses* when the securities are sold. When brokerage fees are paid to sell securities, they are deducted from the proceeds so that brokerage fees to sell securities reduce the net proceeds. This will either decrease a capital gain realized, or increase a capital loss.

Now that you know what can be deducted, know this: many investors wonder if they should leverage existing capital assets in order to invest more into the marketplace. Often they are approached to consider many different leveraged loan arrangements by their financial advisors, particularly if they believe they have not saved enough for retirement.

Some advice: crunch the numbers over the life of the loan. Know how much of a return must be generated every year from the contemplated investment—consistently—for you to pay off your interest (before tax). You will need cash flow to do this. Then, factor your after-tax benefits in. In short: apples to apples, hard cash for hard cash. The investment must be able to pay real dollars on a guaranteed basis before your risk can be properly assessed. You'll be asked to do the same to fund the loan. Your financial advisor needs to speak to this, so that you can sleep at night.

Minimize quarterly instalment payment requirements

If you're one of the many investors who sold leveraged investments at a loss in 2008, you'll be relieved to know that at least a portion of the interest you paid to acquire those investments is deductible. During the time that you owned the investment, the full amount of interest paid to purchase them is a deductible carrying charge. After you disposed of the investment, if the proceeds were not enough to pay off the loan, the interest on the remaining balance is still a deductible carrying charge. You can continue to deduct the interest until the loan is fully repaid. If you did not use the proceeds to pay down the loan, then you can deduct only the portion of interest that would have been paid had you done so.

Taxpayers who have a net tax owing of more than $3,000 in the current tax year and either:

- the previous tax year or
- the second previous tax year

are required to pay their taxes by making instalment payments. For residents of Quebec, the threshold is $1,800.

Farmers and fishermen are permitted to make one instalment of at least two-thirds of the estimated taxes for the year. This payment is due by December 31 of the taxation year. All

Essential TAX FACT #145

It pays to monitor your quarterly instalment payment. Better to invest in yourself all year long, than to overpay the government.

others are required to remit the estimated taxes in quarterly instalments. Due dates are:

- March 15
- June 15
- September 15
- December 15

If the CRA sends you an instalment notice, based on tax owing on your previous filings, there will be no penalties or instalment interest charged so long as you pay the amounts specified by the dates specified on the notice, regardless of whether the amounts properly reflects the taxes due for the year. This is called the "no calc" or "no calculation" method.

Most people don't know there are two other ways to estimate instalment payments: the "current year" and the "prior year" method, which could serve to decrease instalments, thereby freeing up new capital for investment purposes.

If you have been making instalment payments in 2008, review your anticipated income level for 2009 carefully. With the financial turbulence experienced since the fall of 2008, you may find that your overall income from investments, employment and business activities may have taken a hit. You may wish to recalculate required instalments based on either of the following options:

- *Current-year option*—under this option, prepare an estimate of your current year's tax liability, and if the estimate exceeds $3,000 then one-quarter of the estimated amount is due on each of the four due dates. Interest will be charged under this method when taxes prepaid are insufficient or late.

- *Prior-year option*—under this option, total instalments for the year are equal to the net taxes due for the prior year. If the amounts are paid on time throughout the year but insufficient when the return is filed, no interest will be charged.

The interest rate charged by CRA is prescribed quarterly and interest is compounded daily. If one or more instalment payment is late, the interest payable may be offset by making a subsequent payment early. This "contra" interest on the early instalment payment will be used to offset the interest on the late instalment. However, it doesn't work the other way: if CRA has overcollected instalments, no interest is paid out to you.

Penalties for delinquent instalments. When the interest charge payable to CRA is more than $1,000, a penalty is assessed. This penalty is 50% of the interest payable minus the greater of $1,000 and 25% of the instalment interest, calculated as if no instalments had been made for the year. At current rates, instalments of more than approximately $28,000 are needed to reach the threshold for this penalty.

**Essential
TAX FACT #146**

Instalment tax payments are no longer payable on or after the day a taxpayer dies.

CHAPTER REFLECTION:
ESSENTIAL TAX FILING FACTS FOR INVESTORS

1. The more after-tax dollars you have to invest today, the wealthier you'll be in the future.

2. Your net income can be reduced by making contributions to registered accounts such as an RPP and RRSP.

3. When your investment earnings compound on a tax-deferred basis within a registered account, you tap into the most tax efficient way to earn investment income.

4. The tax deduction for your RRSP contribution need not be taken in full in the year you make it—you can choose to defer the deduction into the future.

5. Income from property specifically does not include capital gains or losses from the disposition of such property.

6. Canada's "self assessment" system puts the onus of proof on you, the taxpayer, to prove gross and net income earned.

7. The marginal tax rate is the rate of tax paid on the next dollar earned or saved on the next dollar deducted. Income source, income level and rates of tax applied are needed to calculate this.

8. Income earned on money or assets transferred to your spouse or minor children will usually be "attributed back" to the transferor.

9. The Attribution Rules will apply to joint accounts held by parents and minor children as well as spouses.

10. The Attribution Rules can be avoided in saving for your children's education by investing in an RESP.

11. Many Canadians buy CSBs on a payroll deduction plan, in which case the interest charge paid is deductible on Line 221 as a carrying charge.

12. Accrued interest earned inside a non-registered account is reported annually on the anniversary date of the investment contract.

13. In general when interest rates rise, the value of a bond or debenture paying a fixed rate of interest will decrease, and vice versa.

14. A taxpayer can earn substantial dividends on a tax free basis, depending on the province of residence. But because the dividend "gross up" artificially increases net income, it may reduce refundable or non-refundable tax credits.

15. Income earned on mutual funds will increase their cost base if reinvested, which can affect your eventual gain or loss when you sell them.

16. Within a segregated fund, the policyholder does not own the units; the segregated fund trust does. Therefore income allocations do not affect the value of the fund.

17. Real estate investors can earn investment income, too.

18. It pays to monitor your quarterly instalment payment. It is better to invest in yourself all year long, than to overpay the government.

STAY CURRENT—WHAT'S NEW

Beginning in 2009, the new Tax-Free Savings Account will become available at most financial institutions. Every taxpayer over 17 who filed a 2007 tax return has been allocated $5,000 TFSA contribution room for 2009 and indexed amounts each subsequent year. Contributions up to that limit can be made to a TFSA and any income earned will accumulate tax-free within the account and also when removed from the account. Each family with non-registered investments should be setting up one or more TFSA accounts to shelter that investment income.

The Registered Disability Savings Plan is another new way to accumulate tax-deferred income for 2008 and subsequent years. This plan, which may be set up for any individual who is eligible for the Disability Amount, is designed to provide assistance for disabled taxpayers. Contributions to the plan are not deductible, but are matched by the government, with matching amounts exceeding contributions for moderate-income families. For low-income families, the Canada Disability Savings Bond adds $1,000 a year to the plan, even if no contributions are made.

NOW PUT MORE MONEY IN YOUR POCKET ALL YEAR LONG...

PERSPECTIVE

- To accumulate capital, start a disciplined savings plan today.
- Build equity by first investing in a tax exempt principal residence.
- Reduce non-deductible debt. Try to eliminate interest paid on credit card balances and minimize interest costs on principal residences. Then use your new found cash to invest wisely.
- Split income with family members. Know that better tax results can be achieved for the family unit as a whole when income is distributed amongst the family members. So plan to split income with family members whenever possible, but avoid the Attribution Rules.

- Understand the effects of time and rates of return: $1,000 invested now and then again at the start of each year with a semi-annual compounding frequency will grow to just over $5,500 in 5 years at 4% interest. At 10% that same investment would grow to close to $6,300—14% more. If you hold on to that investment pattern for 25 years, your investment of $1,000 a year will grow to over $42,000 at 4% and over $103,000 at 10%.

- The "Rule of 72" tells us that it will take 18 years for your investment to double at a 4% rate of return—but only 7.2 years at 10%. So rate is very important, especially when the reality of inflation erosion is factored into your investments' performance.

- Earn a bonus with an RRSP. Tax sheltering can help you hedge inflation erosion and give a lift to your rates of return. One of the best ways to do so is through the use of an RRSP. The accumulation results are dramatic. So make that your first priority.

- Be more tax efficient within your non-registered accounts by diversifying your income sources.

ESSENTIAL TAX FACTS FOR WEALTH PRESERVATION

What's important?

Retirement readiness of Canadians in *The Wealth of Canadians: An Overview of the Survey of Financial Security 2005* by Pensions and Wealth Surveys Section of Statistics Canada found that the single most important asset for Canadians was the principal residence, which from a tax planning point of view is a very good thing. That's because gains on one principal residence per family unit is considered to be a tax exempt asset.

This same survey found that mortgage debt is up over 40% since 1999. Given the recent global financial crisis, any type of credit crunch for Canadian families could affect their ability to repay home mortgages, and other personal debt, including amounts owed to the Canada Revenue Agency. An unexpected job loss, illness in the family or other unforeseen event can affect the ability to repay debt; which puts families at financial risk. Therefore, asset protection is important. Knowing how those situations are affected by tax law is important.

Real wealth management—what's left after costs, taxes and inflation—involves a consistent process of earning, saving and preserving your assets on a tax-efficient basis.

Remember, your largest eroder of family wealth will likely be the tax department. There is power in the investment of the tax exempt family residence, because that equity can be leveraged to create new wealth. This is true of investments in the new Tax-Free Savings Account as well.

However, equally important is your opportunity to manage debt, family business transitions, separations, death of a family member and retirement.

In this final section of the book, we'll look at the tax preferences available to manage all of this, and the order in which you should use them so that you, together with your professional advisors—tax accountants, financial planners, lawyers and insurance specialists—can get the after-tax results you need.

Leveraging the ability of your professional team to provide you with the right advice about your family assets, and net worth, can be powerful.

The following Essential Tax Facts are presented with the hope that you'll better understand how to do this, in conjunction with a great relationship with your professional advisors. That begins with your ability to ask probing questions to get the results you want:

1. How much do you need to fund your retirement years?

2. Which assets will you keep, which will you sell to generate capital for your own lifestyle, and which do you plan to pass on?

3. What do you need to know about "arm's length transactions?"

4. Which of your family assets are exempt and which are taxable?

5. Can you safely use your home for personal and business use without compromising your tax exemptions?

6. How do you maximize opportunities to use your home to produce income?

7. What is the tax advantage of a mortgage take-back arrangement?

8. What's the best way to take full advantage of your capital losses?

9. What happens on your tax return when you default on a mortgage?

10. How do separations, divorce and death impact the tax values of your assets?

11. What are the opportunities to withdraw from an RRSP and your TFSA, without penalty and on a tax-free basis?

12. How can you best map your objectives for starting an estate plan?

What's new?

- The New TFSA has consequences on marriage breakdown and death of a taxpayer.

- So does the new RDSP—it's important to review how your new assets will be treated upon sale or deemed disposition.

- It is possible to carry over capital losses from tax year 1972 on the 2008 tax return, provided tax returns to report losses when they occurred were filed.

- Interest paid on investment loans will continue to be tax deductible, even if the value of the asset has diminished.

How much more do you need?

There are two questions individuals ask themselves in planning for their future:

1. How much will I need to retire and

2. How much will I be able to leave my heirs?

These are good questions, and Canadian families have been working hard to find the right answers over the past several years. One of the reasons why today's Canadians are wealthier than generations before is that their financial assets include real estate and private pension accumulations. Increasingly, savings in registered and unregistered accounts are enhancing Canadians' net worth. It is also important to note that for the first time in history women are coming to end of life with their own assets and pensions; all of which adds to this generation's unprecedented wealth.

Still, it is estimated that 90% of Canadians don't top up their available RRSP contribution room. Therefore, shoring up the family RRSP investment is a good place to start for those who wish to take more control of their after tax wealth and plan for a worry free retirement.

Now, with the opportunity to invest in the Tax-Free Savings Account, we have two top investing priorities, at least from a tax planning viewpoint. In what order should we invest? That depends:

1. RRSP First: If you are age eligible, are taxable and have unused RRSP contribution room, make the RRSP contribution first. That will result in double-digit returns on your investment by way of tax savings, and the resulting tax reductions can then be invested into a TFSA.

Essential TAX FACT #147

Canadians could be so much wealthier, if they took full advantage of the most common and lucrative tax preference: the RRSP.

2. The TFSA second: Invest your tax refund into your TFSA—a great way to leverage your refund and benefit from tax exempt earnings, too. Suggest that every working member of your family do the same.

3. The TFSA first: If you have no unused RRSP contribution room, no qualifying earned income and/or are age ineligible for RRSP purposes, or if you are not taxable, put your savings into a TFSA first.

Preparing for a future when you have to count more on your income from your savings can be an especially frightening proposition in turbulent times. Planning helps; so does taking advantage of every single tax preference available. Problem is, most Canadians don't do that. Ask your financial advisors for help in projecting your after-tax income needs. Integrate this with a tax-efficient savings withdrawal plan, especially during periods of change. Your capital will go farther if you take the time to study your tax options before accessing funds in your registered or unregistered accounts or leveraging your investments in real estate.

You may wish to ask some very specific questions: What are your options for preserving assets when you want to transfer them to family members during your lifetime? How are your assets going to be taxed on death or divorce? Should certain assets be disposed of sooner than others? Are there special rules for transfers of assets within the family? Finally, how can you maximize your RRSP withdrawals when it is time to start a retirement annuity?

By planning with a tax focus, your lifetime achievements in accumulating capital will not only support you as you transition into to new life cycles, but you will have an excellent chance of preserving capital which continues to grow while you tap in.

Choose a tax order to preserve capital

Consider your needs carefully before you initiate a taxable disposition of your savings. Are you cashing in to fund a short term financial dilemma, due to marital change or to fund retirement lifestyles? Your reasons for tapping into your capital accumulations will drive the choice of which investments to cash in, and in what order. To preserve your wealth in times of change, think about following a tax efficient order of disposition to "realize" the least amount of taxable income possible.

You may also wish to think of your capital accumulations within three broad categories as you contemplate your options:

1. *Tax exempt assets.* This can include your principal residence and proceeds you will receive from life insurance policies. It may be possible to tap into the equity built up in these assets first, as proceeds will usually be tax exempt. It may also be possible to leverage your equity in these assets, in some cases. Going forward, the new Tax-Free Savings Account could become an important part of your tax exempt assets. Be sure to maximize this opportunity, too.

2. *Tax pre-paid assets.* This includes investments held inside non-registered accounts, like personal property, shares, mutual funds and bonds, and revenue properties. These investments will have been made on a tax pre-paid basis—that is, no tax deduction is allowed when the principal is invested. Depending on asset class, your marginal tax bracket and market timing, it is best to realize profits from these sources on a planned basis, especially in times of change.

3. *Tax-assisted accumulations.* This commonly includes accumulations within registered accounts, such as an RRSP, for which a tax deduction was received when capital was invested. The purpose of this capital is to fund specific lifecycle needs—your retirement, for example—when other actively earned income sources diminish or disappear. Because earnings are sheltered within the plan along the way, it is often, but not always, best to continue the tax deferral as long as possible, to preserve the tax preferences. Tax efficient withdrawal strategies should take into account marginal tax rates during a your lifetime and at death, because unlike other asset dispositions, the withdrawal of capital from an RRSP is fully taxable.

Especially when under pressure, many people think about withdrawing money from their

Essential TAX FACT #148

You might own some tax exempt assets which you can leverage to help with debt. For most people, that includes one principal residence per household. Others own shares of a qualifying small business corporation, which may qualify for a Capital Gains Exemption of up to $750,000. The benefits received from life insurance policies are also tax exempt to the beneficiary.

Essential TAX FACT #149

When you withdraw money from an RRSP, both principal and earnings must be added in full to your income in the year of withdrawal, unless you withdraw under a Home Buyers' Plan or Lifelong Learning Plan.

Essential
TAX FACT #150

RRSP deposits can fund retirement, but also home purchases and post-secondary education too.

Essential
TAX FACT #151

The increase in value in capital assets held outside registered accounts will accrue on a tax deferred basis until they are disposed of. Then only 50% of the gain will be taxable. Losses incurred on most capital assets, however, are only deductible against capital gains, but will qualify for carryover provisions.

RRSPs first. This may or may not be the best place to start.

If you are trying to fund the purchase of a new home or returning to post-secondary school, it could be a good idea, as you can tap into the RRSP on a tax free basis under the Home Buyers' Plan or Lifelong Learning Plans. We'll discuss this in more detail later.

If the lump sum you need is smaller and based on a short term need, (you owe CRA an unexpected balance due, your credit cards are maxed, or you have to pay for a funeral) you may wish to contribute to rather than withdraw from an RRSP, thereby creating new capital with tax savings. This can work if you are age eligible and have the contribution room and may not require any new capital, as you may be able to flip assets held outside registered accounts into an RRSP to create the deduction.

If, on the other hand, the sums you need are large, or if lifecycle changes require asset dispositions due to illness, death, divorce or moves to another city to take a job, you will want to know the special rules on how and when to report capital gains and preserve losses arising on the disposition of other assets.

You may be able to control when you sell or transfer an asset (over two tax years for example) or choose investments that allow you to blend the withdrawal of tax-prepaid principal and taxable earnings—all with the goal of minimizing your overall tax cost.

But, of course, tapping into those significant resources will only work if you are ready to sell, or if in fact, your asset is accessible to you within your required time lines. Investors who feel pressured to sell RRSP assets to shore up shortages in value in their non-registered margin accounts, should look to their various tax-efficient options before doing so. The RRSP withdrawal can in fact exasperate the situation, as it will be taxable, and that will make CRA a creditor, too.

In short, depending on the diversity of your portfolio, your marginal tax rate, and your family tax filing profile, there are several options for income and equity creation to discuss with your financial advisors.

Embrace tax consequences of family asset transfers

To everything there is a season…perhaps it is time to move your ailing parents into your home to better take care of them. Should you sell their home? Perhaps your parents have decided it is time to pass the cottage to you and your siblings. At what value will you inherit this now? Perhaps you have decided to leave the country to take a job overseas. How can you avoid departure taxes if you don't wish to sell your assets?

Many of these real life scenarios result in taxable consequences without the exchange of money. So, to begin any discussion on wealth preservation in times of change, you will need to understand your obligations and opportunities when assets are transferred to family members. To do so, you need to understand some tax jargon:

- "Arm's length" transactions are those undertaken with an unrelated person.

- "Non-arm's length" persons are related to you by blood, marriage or adoption, or those affiliated with you, which can include a common-law partner, corporation, partnership or members of a group who are affiliated with one another.

For example, when Tom sells his rental property to an unrelated third party, he is conducting business on an arm's length basis. If he sells the property to his wife, Samantha, it is a non-arm's length transaction.

The disposal of your assets can be through an actual sale, or upon a "deemed disposition". A deemed disposition arises:

- On death
- When an asset's use is changed from business to personal

> **Essential TAX FACT #152**
>
> Sometimes, assets are sold to strangers or transferred to relatives. In fact, assets can often be transferred without immediate tax consequences to spouses or children. This is called a "tax-free rollover" to a non-arm's length party.

> **Essential TAX FACT #153**
>
> For most assets transferred to a spouse or common-law partner, tax consequences of disposition can be deferred until the asset is actually disposed of.

- When property is transferred to a trust or a registered account
- When you emigrate
- When an asset is given to another as a gift
- When one asset is exchanged for another
- When an asset is stolen, damaged, destroyed or expropriated
- When shares held are converted, redeemed or cancelled
- When options to acquire or dispose of property expire
- When a debt is settled or cancelled.

Essential TAX FACT #154

When assets are transferred to the spouse, income from the property and gains or losses on disposition will be attributed back to the transferor unless the receiving spouse actually pays fair market value for the asset or a bona fide loan is drawn up.

For example, Marion needed to make an RRSP contribution but she had no cash. Instead, she opted to transfer 100 shares of ABC corporation to her self-directed RRSP. Marion will receive an RRSP receipt for the fair market value of the shares and must also report a capital gain—as she is "deemed" to have disposed of the shares at their fair market value.

At the time of sale or transfer, the Adjusted Cost Base of your asset (original cost plus or minus certain adjustments) will be subtracted from the proceeds of disposition to calculate the resulting gain or loss. As transfers between family members generally occur without the exchange of money, a deemed disposition occurs…but at what value?

At the time of such transfers to a spouse, it is only necessary to report the change of ownership on the transferor's return at the asset's adjusted cost base. This results in a "tax-free rollover" of the asset to the spouse.

You can also elect not to have those general rules apply by making an election when filing the return. In that case, the transfer will be reported at the property's fair market value (FMV). The tax consequences will then be addressed immediately on your return—that is, a capital gain or loss could result. Consulting with a tax advisor is wise.

This might be particularly advantageous, for example, if you want to use up capital loss balances. (The same strategy—electing FMV instead of ACB— may be used in transferring assets upon the death of one spouse.)

When you transfer an asset to your spouse at FMV and provided that the spouse pays FMV or a bona fide loan is drawn up:

- income earned from the property is reported by the spouse to whom the property is transferred
- later dispositions of the property will be taxed in the transferee spouse's hands
- interest paid on a loan drawn will be deductible if the resulting property is used to earn income, and interest is actually paid
- you will report that interest received on your tax return.

Note that the gains or losses from the disposition of capital assets transferred to minor children will be included on their own returns—often resulting in nil tax. However transfers of assets to adult children are treated differently.

For example, Harold and Edna want to transfer their cottage property to their adult son Jonathan and his wife Jesse this year. At the time of transfer, fair market value will be assessed, and Harold and Edna will use that figure as the "proceeds of disposition" on their tax return. This will normally produce a taxable gain; however, if the property is a principal residence, a special tax exemption may be tapped.

Essential TAX FACT #155

When you transfer property to your adult children during your lifetime, the property is always transferred at fair market value and the tax consequences are immediately reported. Timing is important.

Taxable and tax-free rollovers may also arise on emigration, separation or divorce or death. Speak to your tax and financial advisors before these changes occur, wherever possible, and understand the tax calculations behind any resulting capital gain and loss applications.

This becomes especially important in 2009 with the new Tax-Free Savings Account, which can be transferred tax free to a spouse on death or divorce.

In the case of the Registered Disability Savings Plan, where the beneficiary dies, or otherwise ceases to qualify for the RDSP, any Canada Disability Savings Grant (CDSG) or Canada Disability Savings Bond (CDSB) funded by government to the plan within the ten years preceding death, and the income earned on such amounts, must be repaid. Amounts in excess of contributions, after taking into account the repayment, will be included in income of the beneficiary in the year of death.

Timing and history are key in understanding capital gains tax

In the last chapter, we focused on capital accumulation and tax efficient income investing along the way. There you learned that the value of a capital asset accrues on a tax deferred basis until disposition—actual or deemed—even when held outside a registered account. For the purpose of the discussion below, we will be focusing on dispositions of those assets held outside of registered accounts.

Essential
TAX FACT #156

There are two unique characteristics of capital assets. The first is that capital gains or losses only arise when an asset is actually disposed of. This leads to the second characteristic: any increase in the value of a qualifying asset while it is held is not taxable until it is disposed of.

When an income-producing asset is disposed of for an amount greater than what its value on acquisition, a capital gain will arise. If an asset is disposed of for less than its original cost, a capital loss is the result.

Although it is usually income-producing assets like stocks, bonds and real estate that fall under the capital gains provisions, certain personal items may also be subject to capital gains tax. This can include second homes, coins, and rare jewellery.

The amount of a capital gain (or loss) is the difference between the proceeds from disposing of the asset and the adjusted cost base (ACB) of that asset, less any outlays and expenses, as outlined in the last chapter.

To refresh your memory use this equation to compute your capital gains or losses:

$$\text{Proceeds of Disposition} - \text{Adjusted Cost Base} - \text{Outlays and Expenses} = \text{Capital Gain or Loss}$$

The amount of capital gain that is included in income is called the "taxable gain" and this is determined by the capital gains inclusion rate. This has changed a number of times since the introduction of capital gains taxes in 1972, as outlined below:

History of Capital Gains Inclusion Rates

- 1972-1987 and Oct. 18, 2000 to date: 50% (½)
- 1988-89 and Feb. 28, 2000 to Oct. 17, 2000   66.67% (⅔)
- 1990-Feb. 27, 2000   75% (¾)

Because the capital gains inclusion rate changed in 2000, it was possible to have a "blended capital gains inclusion rate" for that year, varying from 50% to 75% depending on when any capital gains or losses were experienced during the year.

In certain cases, when you dispose of capital assets, you may not have to include capital gain in your income. For example, when you donate publicly traded shares to a registered charity or private foundation, your capital gains inclusion rate is deemed to be zero—you get a donation credit for the value of the shares but you don't have to pay any tax on the gain! In cases where you dispose of a capital asset that is being used in a business and replace the asset with another, you may be able to defer any capital gains on the original asset until the replacement is disposed of.

Why do you need to know this? Simply stated, to apply your capital losses properly.

When a capital disposition ends in a loss, it must first be applied to reduce all other capital gains income of the year on Schedule 3. If a taxable capital gain remains, it is reported as income at Line 127 of the return.

When you bring forward an unused loss from a prior year (incurred in the period 1972 to present) it may be necessary to adjust the loss to today's capital gains inclusion rate—50%.

> **Essential**
> **TAX FACT #157**
>
> Capital losses may only be used to reduce capital gains in the current year. If losses exceed gains in the current year they may be carried back to reduce capital gains in any of the previous three years or in any subsequent year.

One more important tax concept to note: the way in which capital losses are applied may differ, depending on the type of asset you own.

Manage disposition of your tax prepaid assets

When you acquire assets outside of a registered account, you must classify the asset properly for tax purposes. There are several categories of capital properties on Schedule 3 of the tax return, which is completed in the year you dispose of such assets. These include:

- Personal use property
- Listed personal property
- Small business corporation shares

- Identical properties such as mutual funds, publicly traded shares, bonds

- Real estate and other depreciable property

Personal use property. This is property you hold primarily for personal use and enjoyment, or the use and enjoyment of your family. This includes such items as a car, boat, cottage, furniture, and other personal effects.

The $1,000 Rule states that both the proceeds and adjusted cost base of the property are recorded as at least $1,000. This rule effectively ignores accounting for gains on smaller personal-use items.

Losses on personal-use property (other than listed personal property) are deemed to be nil because they are considered to be a personal cost of owning the asset. For example, if you own a cottage for personal use and enjoyment, and sell that cottage at a loss, there are no tax consequences. Personal residence dispositions are discussed in more detail later.

There is a special rule that prevents you from claiming the $1,000 minimum ACB on each piece of a set of properties.

For example, assume a couple wishes to sell a set of silver goblets and cutlery to make enough money for a trip to Cuba. The set was acquired for $750 at a garage sale and the couple can now sell each piece for $50. There are 100 pieces in the set. The set is considered to be one property and the $1,000 rule will apply only once to the entire sales transaction, even if the pieces are sold to multiple buyers over a period of time. Thus, the proceeds of disposition for the entire set will be $5,000 and the adjusted cost base of the entire set will be $1,000.

Listed personal property. This is a special subset of personal-use property which includes collectible pieces such as:

- a print, etch, drawing, painting, sculpture, or other similar work of art,

- jewellery,

- a rare folio, rare manuscript or rare book,
- a stamp, or
- a coin or coin collection.

As with other personal-use property, gains on listed personal property are taxable as capital gains on Schedule 3, and are subject to the $1,000 Rule. However, losses on these properties are treated differently.

Essential TAX FACT #160

Losses on listed personal property are allowed, but may only be deducted from gains on other listed personal property.

Where losses on listed personal property exceed gains reported during the year from other listed personal property, unused balances may be carried back and applied against listed personal property gains in any of the prior three years or carried forward to apply against listed personal property gains in any of the following seven years.

Let's now turn our discussion to the disposition of a special type of personal use property, held by the majority of Canadian taxpayers: personal residences which can include a principal residence and one or more vacation properties.

Maximize lucrative tax exemptions for personal residences

Under Canadian tax law, the principal residence is a very important concept. Under current rules, each household (adult taxpayer and/or spouse) can designate one principal residence to be tax exempt on sale. A principal residence is classified to be "personal-use property", which means that any losses on disposition are deemed to be nil (that's right, not claimable on the tax return).

Essential TAX FACT #161

In most cases, any capital gain on the disposition of a principal residence will be exempt from tax.

A principal residence can include a house, cottage, condo, duplex, apartment, or trailer that is ordinarily inhabited by you or some family member at some time during the year. Except where the principal residence is a share in a co-operative housing corporation, the principal residence also includes the land immediately subjacent to the housing unit

Essential TAX FACT #162

If you have had only one principal residence, used solely for personal use, no tax reporting is required at the time of disposition, even if a capital gain results.

and up to one-half hectare of adjacent property that contributes to the use of the housing unit as a residence. If the lot size exceeds one-half hectare, it may be included in the principal residence if it can be shown to be necessary for the use of the housing unit.

Where a family owns *only one property* and lived in the property every year while they owned it, the calculation of the tax exemption on disposition of the property is very straightforward. In these cases there won't be any taxable capital gain on the property.

Where *more than one property* is owned, and the family uses both residences at some time during the year, the calculation of the principal residence exemption becomes slightly more difficult when one property is disposed of.

For periods including 1971 to 1981, each spouse can declare one of the properties as their principal residence. This means that any capital gain that accrued in this period can be sheltered on both properties provided that each was owned by a different spouse.

This effectively means that after 1981 any accrued capital gain on one of the properties (that isn't designated as a principal residence) will be ultimately subject to tax when sold.

The following are important dates to know when assessing the tax consequences of the disposition of family residences:

- *Pre 1972:* no tax will be levied on accrued gains on any capital assets

- *1972 to 1981:* one tax-exempt principal residence allowed in the hands of each spouse

- *1982 to date:* one tax-exempt principal residence allowed to each family unit where there was legal married status

- *1993 to date:* one tax-exempt principal residence allowed to each conjugal relationship (common-law)

- *1998 to 2001:* same-sex couples could elect conjugal status, thereby limiting their tax exempt residences to one per unit

- *2001 to date:* same-sex couples required to recognize one tax-exempt principal residence per conjugal relationship.

In a nutshell, the capital gain on the property is first calculated using regular rules for capital gains and losses. Once this has been done, the exempt portion is calculated, and this exempt portion is subtracted from the capital gain. The exempt portion of the gain is calculated as:

$$\text{Total Gain} \quad X \quad \frac{(\text{Number of years designated as principal residence} + 1)}{\text{Number of years the property was owned}}$$

For example, assume the Smith family sold a cottage last year. They designated it to be their principal residence for nine of the ten years in which they owned it. As a result, they paid no taxes on the gain they earned on disposition. This year, however, they are selling their home in the city. This property will be designated the principal residence for 11 of the 20 years they owned it, as the cottage was designated the principal residence in the other nine years.

To calculate the exempt portion of the gain on the second property, the capital gain is multiplied by the formula: 11 years of designated ownership plus one year divided by 20 years (the number of years the property was owned). *Form T2091* would be used to make this calculation and the resulting capital gain would be reported on Schedule 3 of the tax return.

It's most important for anyone who made a capital gains election on capital assets in 1994 to file *Form T664 Capital Gains Election* with their will so that executors can take that 1994 valuation into account on the disposition of assets on the final return.

**Essential
TAX FACT #165**

The taxable capital gain arrived at on *Form T2091*, is further reduced by any capital gains election made to use up the $100,000 Capital Gains Deduction on February 22, 1994. It is important to be aware of this election, especially if you are the executor of an estate.

Mixed Use of Principal Residence. When you start using a principal residence for income-producing (rental, home office) purposes, "change of use" rules must be observed for tax purposes.

Essential
TAX FACT #166

When a principal residence is converted from personal use to income-producing use, an election may be made to ignore the deemed disposition rules normally required under the change of use rules explained above.

Essential
TAX FACT #167

A property may be designated a principal residence for up to four years after moving out; sometimes longer.

Essential
TAX FACT #168

It is also possible to make a special election when you convert a rental property to a principal residence.

- *The fair market value* of the property must be assessed. This is because for tax purposes you are deemed to have disposed of the property and immediately reacquired it at the same fair market value, changing its classification from a personal-use property to an income-producing property. However, two separate elections may be made under certain circumstances to avoid an immediate tax problem. See Tax Facts #166 and #167.

- *The resulting capital gain*, if any, is nil if the home is designated in each year as a principal residence. However, any taxable gain would be calculated on *Form T2091* if you owned and designated a second property to be your principal residence at any time the first property was owned.

- If at some time in the future, the property is converted back to use as a principal residence, the same FMV assessment must be made, as you are deemed to have disposed of and reacquired the property for this new use. Tax consequences are then assessed, possibly resulting in a capital gain or a loss. Note that the portion of the loss relating to the land (but not the building) would be allowed because during this period, the property was not personal-use property. No capital loss can be claimed on a depreciable property, such as a building, although a terminal loss that arises may be claimed.

If you have elected to defer recognizing the change in use of the property, any capital gain or loss will only be accounted for when you actually sell the property, or when you choose to rescind the election.

You can choose to designate the property as your personal residence for up to four years after moving; longer if it was a requirement of your employer that you relocate to a temporary residence that is at least 40 kilometres away. This extension will be allowed where you move back into the home on which the designation is being made before the end of the calendar year in which employment is terminated.

How do you accomplish all of this?

Simply attach a letter to the tax return in the year of the property changes to an income-producing use, noting that a *S. 45(2) Election* is being made. Attach a description of the property itself and sign the election. And be very careful to observe these additional rules:

Essential TAX FACT #169

When a principal residence is used in part for business purposes (home office, child care enterprises, etc.), it is possible to retain the principal residence exemption status, provided that no capital cost allowance is claimed on the property.

- Any rental income earned on the property while you are absent must be reported in the normal manner.

- Capital Cost Allowance must not be claimed on the property. If it is, you will lose your principal residence exemption on the portion of the property upon which this deduction is claimed.

- No other property can be designated as a principal residence at the same time.

- You must have been a resident or deemed resident of Canada.

Similarly, you can defer accounting for the deemed disposition when an income-producing property converts to personal use, by making a similar election. This is only allowable, however, if no capital cost allowance was claimed on the property since 1984. Follow the same election procedures as described above, but cite *S. 45(3)*.

Optimize tax rules on other real estate holdings

The disposition of real property can be very lucrative, often depending on its timing, and its use. So, it can pay off handsomely to know the tax rules before you act. The term 'real estate' usually includes buildings and land, but can also include a leasehold interest in real property.

When you hold real estate for your personal use and enjoyment, for example, it will generally not earn income, and any gain on sale may be entirely tax exempt if it has always been used as a principal residence, as explained above. In the case of second or subsequent residences that do not produce income, a capital gain would generally be reportable on disposition.

The disposition of income-producing real estate, therefore, can produce either:

- a capital gain (or loss—but only on land) which is 50% taxable under current rules, if property has been used to produce income (generally rents) or

- income from a business, which is fully taxable. This might occur when the property itself is classified as inventory, as in the subdivision and sale of lots.

Real Estate Held as an Income-Producing Investment. When real estate is held to produce rental income, any increase in value is considered to be capital in nature and capital gains treatment will prevail. However, the calculations on disposition can be a bit tricky, as the building is considered to be a "depreciable property", while the land is not.

As depreciable property, buildings used in the course of your rental enterprise or business are eligible for a deduction under the Capital Cost Allowance (CCA) rules. These rules account for the loss of value of an asset over time. Buildings usually generate a deduction of 4% of the asset's undepreciated capital cost (UCC) each year, as they are usually included in Class 1. The cost of the building entered in that class will include its component parts, such as heating, light fixtures, air conditioning, sprinkler systems, etc.

When an income-producing building is acquired, special reporting rules must be followed:

- Acquisition is considered to have occurred when legal title is acquired, or after the property actually exists, whichever comes first.

Essential TAX FACT #170

Should a personal use property change to an income-producing one, a tax consequence would occur on its change of use (at fair market value), and then again on subsequent disposition.

- For possessions after 1989, the asset must be "available for use" in order for CCA to be claimed.

- No CCA deduction is available on the cost of land; therefore the value of the building must be separated from the total cost to schedule the asset properly for CCA purposes.

- When a building is acquired and then immediately torn down, no CCA deduction is allowed as the entire cost is allocated to the value of the land.

- If you own more than one rental property, it is necessary to set up buildings valued at $50,000 or more in separate CCA classes, rather than to pool the assets together in one class.

- Capital cost allowance deductions are limited to the net income from rental properties; that is, losses cannot be created or increased with CCA claims.

- In the year the building is acquired, only half the normal CCA claim may be made—regardless of when during the year the building was acquired.

Tax Fact #171 explains an important rule. Separate calculations may be required to determine the tax consequences of each the land and the building. As well there may be a "recapture" of capital cost allowance deductions claimed on the building. In other cases, a capital loss may occur on the land and a "terminal loss" on the building.

> **Essential**
> **TAX FACT #171**
>
> When a building is disposed of, the proceeds must be allocated to the land and building as well as other depreciable property.

A terminal loss is a deduction that must be claimed where the value of the building declined during its period of ownership more rapidly than was reflected in the CCA claimed. When this happens, a deduction must be made against income in full to account for the actual depreciation of the asset.

This is a significant tax advantage in the year the loss occurs. When land and buildings are sold, CRA wants to ensure that allocations made to land and building are not skewed to create such an advantage.

Therefore, when the proceeds of disposition allocated to the land exceed its cost, (thereby creating a gain) and the proceeds allocated to the building are less than the Undepreciated Capital Cost (UCC) of the building (thereby creating a fully deductible terminal loss) CRA requires an adjustment.

The lesser of:

- the gain on the land and
- the loss on the building

is added to the proceeds from the disposition of the building. The same amount is then subtracted from the proceeds of disposition of the land.

For example, Jim sells a property for $100,000. The property was acquired for $70,000 several years ago. At that time, Jim allocated $60,000 in value to the building and $10,000 to the land. He did not claim a deduction for CCA on the building in the meantime.

Jim decides to allocate $90,000 of the proceeds of disposition to the land (thereby creating an $80,000 capital gain, half of which is taxable), and $10,000 to the building (thereby creating a $50,000 terminal loss, all of which is deductible). The net result would be a $10,000 net deduction which would offset other income in the year.

Even if this allocation reflects fair market value, it is not allowed. The loss on the building is added to its proceeds of disposition, and deducted from the land proceeds, which would result in the elimination of the terminal loss and a reduction of the capital gain to $30,000 (of which half is taxable). You will likely want to get some help from a professional in making your allocations on the sale of your rental properties.

**Essential
TAX FACT #172**

The more closely your business or occupation (e.g. a builder, a real estate agent) is related to real estate transactions, the more likely it is that any gain realized from such a transaction will be considered to be business income rather than a capital gain.

Real Estate Held for Capital Appreciation. When real estate is used in a commercial enterprise, resulting asset dispositions could fall into a grey area. The big question is this: will resulting gains be considered income (100% taxable) rather than capital (50% taxable) in nature?

In deciding on whether a transaction is "income" or "capital" in nature, the courts have considered the following facts on a case-by-case basis:

- the taxpayer's intention with respect to the real estate at the time of its purchase,

- feasibility of the taxpayer's intention,

- geographical location and zoned use of the real estate acquired,

- extent to which these intentions were carried out by the taxpayer,

- evidence that the taxpayer's intention changed after purchase of the real estate,

- the nature of the business, profession, calling or trade of the taxpayer and associates,

- the extent to which borrowed money was used to finance the real estate acquisition and the terms of the financing, if any, arranged,

- the length of time throughout which the real estate was held by the taxpayer,

- the existence of persons other than the taxpayer who share interests in the real estate,

- the nature of the occupation of the other persons who share interest as well as their stated intentions and courses of conduct,

- factors which motivated the sale of the real estate, and

- evidence that the taxpayer and/or associates had dealt extensively in real estate.

Essential TAX FACT #173

Special rules apply to the disposition of vacant land.

Essential TAX FACT #174

It is CRA's view that the subdivision of farmland or inherited land in order to sell it will not necessarily constitute a conversion to inventory.

In summary, if your intention is to earn income from the sale of real estate, the profit is fully included in income from business. However, if the property is held for use in the business (i.e. to produce income) the gain on sale is capital in nature.

Vacant land that is capital property used by its owner for the purpose of gaining or producing income will be considered to have been converted to inventory (and therefore subject to business income computation) at the earlier of :

- the time when the owner commences improvements with a view to selling the property, and

- the time an application is made for approval of subdivision into lots for sale, provided that the taxpayer proceeds with the development of the subdivision.

Mortgage Take Back Arrangements. Sometimes when a property is sold, the vendor takes back a mortgage. The entire transaction must be reported in the year of disposition, but if the full proceeds of sale are not received, a "reserve" can be created to exclude from income the amount due in the future.

The basic calculation works as follows and is made on *Form T2017* before the figures are entered on Schedule 3 of the tax return:

$$\frac{\text{Proceeds not due until after the tax year}}{\text{Total proceeds of disposition}} \times \text{Capital Gain} = \text{Reserve}$$

The capital gains reserve you can claim for amounts not yet received is limited to 5 years for all properties other than family farm or fishing property and small business corporation shares (see below).

The maximum percentage of the gain that may be claimed as a reserve is 80% in the first year, 60% in the second, 40% in the third, 20% in the fourth, and in the fifth year, no reserve may be claimed. In each year, the reserve claimed cannot exceed the reserve claimed in the previous year.

For family farm and fishing property and small business corporation shares transferred to a child, the maximum reserve period is 10 years. The maximum percentage of the gain that may be claimed as a reserve is 90% in the first year, decreasing by 10% each year so that in the tenth year, no reserve may be taken.

So, what happens when you need to sell or transfer your properties and the result is a loss in value, rather than a profit? It's important to understand how to claim those losses over a period of years.

Claim capital losses properly to preserve wealth

There may be a silver lining to that dark cloud of loss. As you have gleaned from our discussions so far, certain types of losses on capital property owned outside of registered accounts may provide tax advantages. In fact, losses that are not deductible in the year incurred may be carried over to other taxation years in certain cases.

Note that the Income Tax Act gives CRA the power to refuse loss recognition if you don't record them on a timely basis. So, you'll always want to recognize those losses on your tax return in the year they occur even though you may not be able to take advantage of the loss in that year. *Form T1A Request for Loss Carryback* is available to help you carry over a loss.

More good news: CRA will begin paying interest on any refund owed to you 30 days after the later of:

- The day on which an application is received
- The day on which an amended return is filed
- The day on which a written request is received
- The first day immediately following the year after the year a loss was incurred.

With the exception of losses on Listed Personal Property, capital losses incurred in the current year must be applied first against capital gains in the current year. When losses completely offset gains in the current year, any remaining loss becomes a "net capital loss" available for carry over.

Note that when the taxpayer dies, unused capital losses can no longer be carried forward so the unused capital losses (reduced by any capital gains deduction previously claimed) may be used to offset other types of income in the year of death or the immediately preceding year.

Net capital losses of other years are deducted on Line 253 of your return.

Note: A special rule applies when investors invest in a limited partnership and lose money.

Essential TAX FACT #177

Net capital losses may be carried back to reduce capital gains reported in any of the previous three taxation years. Amounts that are not applied to prior years may be carried forward indefinitely to apply against capital gains in future years.

Essential TAX FACT #178

Limited partnership losses not claimed at death expire.

Limited partnership income is generally reported to the investor on *Form T5013* and transferred to the tax return on Line 122 or as rent or other investment income, depending on its source. The partner's at-risk amount is shown on the T5013 slip, together with the partner's income or loss from the partnership. This slip will also note what portion of that loss is a limited partnership loss.

Limited partnership losses up to the partner's "at-risk amount" may be deducted against other income. However, when losses exceed the at-risk amount, they cannot be used to offset other income or be carried back. Instead, they must be carried forward until the taxpayer reports limited partnership income. In that year, limited partnership losses of other years are deducted on Line 251 of the tax return.

Report dispositions of shareholdings with acumen

A taxpayer-investor may hold shares of public or privately held corporations and the tax consequences will differ for each.

Public Corporate Holdings. When looking at your holdings of public company shares, it is necessary to determine whether you owned "identical properties"—that is, shares in public companies or units in a mutual fund that have identical rights and which cannot be distinguished one from the other.

If you do add the cost of all identical shares in the group and divide the sum by the number of shares held to determine the average cost per share.

Essential TAX FACT #179

When you trade some of a group of identical shares, you must calculate an average cost each time there is a purchase, in order to report a capital gain or loss on Schedule 3 properly.

For example, assume Leila purchased 1,000 shares of XYZ company on June 1 and then another 800 shares on August 31. In the first case she paid $10 per share and in the second she paid $12.00 per share. She now owns 1,800 shares for an average cost of $10.89 ([1,000 x $10 + 800 x $12] / [1,000 + 800]).

This is important information in October of the same year, when Leila decides to sell 500 shares to finance her Christmas purchases. At that time she gets $15.00 per share and earns a capital gain of:

$7,500 ($15.00 x 500 shares)
− $5,445 ($10.89 x 500)

= $2,055 before brokerage fees

Leila may have wanted to time her winners and losers for maximum tax advantages. That is, she could plan to offset her capital gains from this transaction with capital losses generated through "tax loss selling"—the timing of the sale of capital property which has an unrealized capital loss, so that the loss may be used to offset realized capital gains.

For example, Leila might choose to sell her shares in ABC Company, held outside her RRSP, which she bought for $9 a share and which are currently worth $6 per share. That capital loss will be offset against her gains from XYZ company if the transaction occurred in the same year.

There is no restriction to this type of transaction, except where prope
identical to the property which is sold at a loss is purchased within 3(
prior to the disposition, or within 30 days after the disposition. Such
"superficial loss" will be disallowed and is generally added to the Adjusted
Cost Base of the replacement property.

Maximize family capital gains deductions

Certain types of capital gains may be received tax free under a provision
called the Capital Gains Exemption. Gains on the disposition of shares of
qualified small business corporations, qualified farm property and qualified
fishing property qualify. (In 1994 a $100,000 Exemption, available for most
capital property was eliminated, but taxpayers were allowed to make an
election to shelter any gains accrued prior to the elimination date of the
deduction: February 22, 1994).

As of March 19, 2007 the previous lifetime limit of $500,000 was increased
to $750,000. Dispositions prior to March 19, 2007 qualify for the $500,000
amount. Dispositions after March 18 qualify for the new $750,000 amount,
less any deduction previously claimed.

Private Corporate Holdings. The Income Tax Act provides for unique tax
treatment on the disposition of privately held shares of a Qualified Small
Business Corporation (QSBC). To qualify, the shares must be shares of a
small business corporation that was owned by you, your spouse or common-
law partner, or a partnership related to you, and:

- The corporation must have actively used at least 90% of its assets (on a
  fair market value basis) in the operation of the business,

- During the 24 month period prior to the disposition, at least 50% of
  the corporation's assets (on a fair market value basis) must have been
  used in an active business carried on pri-
  marily in Canada,

- During the 24 month period prior to
  disposition, the shares must have been
  shares in a Canadian controlled private
  corporation (CCPC).

The capital gain is reported in the first section
of Schedule 3 and the deduction is claimed on
Form T657 Capital Gains Deduction and Line
254 of the return.

Essential TAX FACT #180

Should a disposition of a
qualified small business
corporation result in a capital
gain, a lifetime capital gains
exemption of $750,000 may
be available.

Dispositions that result in losses are also eligible for special tax treatment. If losses arise on the disposition of shares in a small business corporation or its insolvency, 50% of these can be used to offset all other income of the current year, (use line 217 of the tax return). Should excess losses remain, they can be carried forward back to offset other income of the previous three years or carried forward for a period of 10 years (losses incurred before 2004 can only be carried forward 7 years). Unapplied losses after this period become capital losses, which can be carried forward and applied against capital gains earned in the future.

These are very lucrative tax provisions that can substantially increase the wealth of corporate small business owners, or ease the pain of the loss if times go bad.

Farming and Fishing. The $750,000 lifetime Capital Gains Exemption may also be available to offset a capital gain on the disposition of qualified farm and fishing properties. To be considered to be qualified property, the property must be one of the following:

- An interest in a family farm or fishing partnership owned by you or your spouse or common-law partner,
- Shares in a family farm or fishing corporation owned by you or your spouse or common-law partner,
- Real property (i.e. land, buildings) and eligible capital property (such as quotas) that were used
  - in the business of farming or fishing by you, your spouse (or common-law partner), child, or parent in the preceding 24 months prior to disposition. Gross farming or fishing income must also exceed income from all other sources for at least two years, or
  - by a family farm or fishing corporation or a family farm or fishing partnership of you, your spouse, common-law partner, child or parent that has farming as a principal business for at least 24 months prior to the disposition.

Take a no-surprises approach to interest deductibility and debt forgiveness

Taxpayers often borrow money to make investments that produce income. Is the interest deductible? There are specific tax rules to note.

First, read Tax Fact #181. Other important tax facts to note on interest deductibility include the following:

- Interest on money borrowed to invest in property generating tax-exempt income or an interest in a life insurance policy is specifically not deductible.

- Interest paid on money borrowed to invest may not be deductible at all if there is no reasonable expectation of profit from the investment.

CRA's views on interest deductibility are set out in an Interpretation Bulletin (IT-533). This should be required reading for all tax-payers who borrow money for business or investment purposes and pay interest costs.

Essential TAX FACT #181

Interest incurred when money is borrowed to make an investment in a capital asset is only deductible when the property is acquired for the purposes of earning income (interest, dividends, rents or royalties) or where there is potential for such income to be earned.

Here are the essential tax facts to know:

- *Tracing/linking.* The onus is on you to trace funds to a current and eligible usage.

- *Chief source of income.* The investment loan that gives rise to the interest expense can be for an ancillary, rather than primary, income-producing purpose. This is a question of fact.

- *Borrowing to acquire common shares.* Interest on money borrowed to purchase common shares will be deductible if there is a reasonable expectation at the time the shares were acquired that dividends will be received.

- *Money borrowed to redeem shares or return capital.* Interest will be deductible if the capital replaced was previously used for an income-producing purpose.

- *Borrowing to pay dividends.* The interest will be deductible.

- *Borrowing to make loans to employees and shareholders.* Interest will be deductible by the employer as such loans are viewed as a form of remuneration.

Essential TAX FACT #182

Interest deductibility will hinge upon the direct and current use of the money borrowed and the identification of an income-earning purpose.

- *Borrowing to contribute capital in a company.* Interest may be deductible if the borrowed funds can be linked to an income-producing purpose (e.g. the issuing of dividends). There is a general presumption that if you borrow to buy common shares you are doing so in anticipation of receiving dividends, so any related interest will be deductible.

- *Leveraged buy-outs.* As noted above, interest paid on funds borrowed to acquire common shares will be deductible.

Debt Forgiveness. Investors can sometimes get squeezed in hot real estate markets, running into difficulty with their lenders. The same thing can happen when market values of securities held dip significantly leaving investors with diminished values. Where a debt is forgiven and a debtor is required to pay an amount less than the actual amount owing, there are a series of tax consequences. The forgiven amount is generally applied to reduce a number of other tax preferences. 50% of any remaining balance of the forgiven debt is added to your income.

In order, the forgiven amount is used to reduce:

- Non-capital loss balances (except for allowable business investment losses)
- Farm losses
- Restricted farm losses
- Net capital losses
- Depreciable property's capital cost and UCC balances
- Cumulative eligible capital
- Resource expenditure balances
- Adjusted cost base of certain capital properties
- Current year capital losses.

After these applications are made, 50% of the unapplied forgiven amount is added to income, but a special reserve can be used to minimize tax consequences. When net

Essential
TAX FACT #183

A deduction for the costs of interest and property taxes paid on undeveloped land is limited to net income from the property. Should there be little or no income from the land, undeducted amounts may be added to the cost base of the land, which will affect the size of future capital gains or losses on disposition.

Essential
TAX FACT #184

It is also possible to transfer unused balances of forgiven debt to another taxpayer. Where this is done the debt forgiveness rules described above apply to the other taxpayer.

income is less than $40,000 a year, a deferral of tax is possible. Speak to your tax advisor about these rules. Inquire about whether it is possible for you to continue to write off interest expenses on outstanding loans.

Implement tax preferred separations and final departures

Departure from an existing lifestyle, which gives rise to a capital disposition, can happen as a result of a number of personal changes including:

- Separation or divorce
- Death of the taxpayer.

In each case there is a deemed disposition of capital assets. However, in the case of marriage breakdown, a tax-free rollover is available. Here are some essential tax facts.

Separation and Divorce. A couple need not be legally or formally separated for their tax status to change. A couple is considered to be separated if they cease co-habitation for a period of at least 90 days. When a couple separates:

- Each person will be taxed as an individual
- Income and assets will be separated
- Refundable and non-refundable tax credits will be allocated based on individual net income levels
- Spousal RRSP contributions will no longer be allowed
- Income attribution becomes a non-issue. That is, income attribution ends when there is a separation, providing that an election to this effect is made in the year of separation or after separation, and providing that the couple continues to live apart. Therefore the new owner of the property after a relationship breakdown is responsible for all subsequent tax consequences on the earnings and capital appreciation (depreciation) of the property.
- RRSP accumulations can be split. Funds that have accumulated in RRSPs may be rolled over on a tax free basis to the ex-spouse when the parties are living apart and if the payments follow a written separation agreement, court order, decree or judgement. The transfer must be made directly between the RRSP plans of the two spouses and one spouse cannot be disqualified because of age (over age 71). The same rules for tax-free transfer of funds apply to RRIF accumulations. *Form T2220* is used to authorize the transfers between the plans.

- TFSA accumulations can also be split on a tax-free basis. The funds from one party's TFSA may be transferred tax-free to the other party's TFSA. This will have no effect on the contribution room of either of the parties.

- Property brought into the marriage by one of the spouses will be considered owned by that person. Generally the property is assigned to that person during the negotiation of the separation agreement.

- *Transfer of other property.* Property can be transferred on relationship dissolution at its adjusted cost base, (or Undepreciated Capital Cost in the case of depreciable property) so that there are no tax consequences at the time of transfer. This applies to property transferred in settlement of marital property rights as well as any other voluntary transfers. These rules effectively transfer any accrued gains on the property to the transferee.

Essential
TAX FACT #185

By special election, assets may be transferred at their Fair Market Value. This could result in significant tax savings if, for example, the transferor had unused capital losses to apply to gains on the transferred property.

Please read Tax Fact #185. Where this election is made, the transferee receives a significant tax benefit in that future capital gains will be calculated based on the FMV at the time of transfer. Further, if the FMV of the property is less than its ACB, it may be advantageous to trigger the capital loss. This would allow the transferor to offset other capital gains of the year, the previous three years or capital gains realized in the future.

- Also remember to take into account any capital gains election the individuals may have made in February 1994 and apply the increased adjusted cost base in calculating the tax consequences of property transfers resulting from the relationship breakdown.

- After separation, CRA recognizes two family units, and therefore it is possible for each to own one tax exempt principal residence.

Final Departure. Death generates numerous tax consequences which can be expensive, particularly for single taxpayers (see Part Four). In terms of wealth preservation, however, the acquisition of a life insurance policy can make some sense and can lead to numerous tax advantages, especially if deemed dispositions of capital assets result in a hefty tax bill.

For example, if Judy decides to take out a $100,000 insurance policy on herself and name her baby Jane as beneficiary, her premiums will not be deductible. However, when Judy dies, Jane receives the benefits under the policy tax free.

Sometimes an investment in an insurance policy can result in taxable income. This will happen on the anniversary day of the policy when accumulating funds within certain policies exceed the policy's adjusted cost basis. The amounts must be reported on an annual accrual basis, but a deduction for any over-accrual can be taken when a taxpayer disposes of an interest in the policy.

Income earned within whole life or universal life insurance policies will generally accumulate on a tax-exempt basis provided that the policies have a limitation on the size of the investment component. These features should be discussed with your insurance advisor. The proceeds from a life insurance policy can help to pay the taxes which arise on the deemed disposition of taxable assets as at the date of death.

Essential TAX FACT #186

When an individual buys an insurance policy, the premium is not deductible. But, subsequent benefits or proceeds paid out to beneficiaries are tax exempt.

Essential TAX FACT #187

The investment portion of an insurance policy, known as the Cash Surrender Value (CSV), can be withdrawn by the policy holder. When that happens there is a disposition and there may be tax consequences.

It makes sense to prepare early for your terminal wealth by assessing the place of life insurance in your estate plans.

Leverage your RRSP with tax free withdrawals

"The RRSP is for me, the life insurance is for the kids!"

This is how many taxpayers think of their retirement and estate planning activities and this can have some merit. In fact, it can make some sense to fund a life insurance policy with the tax savings earned from an RRSP contribution!

Investors generally withdraw money from their RRSPs on a taxable basis to create a monthly pension, or to supplement income in periods of unemployment or maternity leave. The idea is to try to withdraw to supplement your financial requirements with the taxable RRSP withdrawal when other income sources end or are interrupted. It makes less sense to withdraw when marginal tax rates are high... unless of course your stellar savings efforts throughout your lifetime have made you a very wealthy person!

It pays to play with a time line and by knowing your marginal tax bracket and rates. As "ordinary income" that is 100% taxable, plan to defer RRSP withdrawals to a new tax year or take money from a lower earner's deposits first, as a way to minimize tax.

But also consider whether you will be in a higher marginal tax bracket at death...if so taxable withdrawals during life can be the most tax efficient RRSP withdrawal strategy.

Essential
TAX FACT #188

The RRSP Home Buyers' Plan allows first time home buyers (or those who have not owned a home in the current year or preceding four years) to withdraw up to $20,000 of funds saved within RRSP for the purpose of buying or building a home, on a completely tax-free basis.

More on creating a tax efficient pension later. However, here's an important fact: amounts withdrawn from an RRSP are taxable in the year received unless the amount is withdrawn under the Lifelong Learning Plan (LLP) or the Home Buyers' Plan (HBP).

The RRSP can be so much more than a tax assisted retirement savings plan. It can help you buy a new home or invest in yourself by going back to school.

HPB withdrawals may be a single amount or the taxpayer may make a series of withdrawals throughout the year as long as the total does not exceed $20,000.

The funds must be repaid back into the RRSP though, over a 15-year period, beginning in the second calendar year after the withdrawal. Amounts which are due and not repaid are included in your income in the year they are due.

It is not necessary that you actually use the funds borrowed for the intended purpose, only that you buy or build the qualifying home.

You and your spouse or common-law partner may each participate in the plan and together withdraw up to $40,000 ($20,000 each) from your RRSPs.

A qualifying home is a housing unit located in Canada. This includes existing homes and those being constructed. Single-family homes, semi-detached homes, townhouses, mobile homes, condominium units, and apartments in duplexes, triplexes, fourplexes, or apartment buildings, all qualify. A share in a co-operative housing corporation that entitles you to possess, and gives you an equity interest in, a housing unit located in Canada also qualifies.

Other essential tax facts include the following:

- *You must file a return.* Members of the Home Buyers' Plan must file a tax return each year until their HBP balance is zero, regardless of whether they are otherwise required to file.

Essential TAX FACT #189

If you contribute to an RRSP in the 90-day period prior to making the HBP withdrawal, and any of the deposit is withdrawn, you may not claim an RRSP deduction for the amount of the contribution which was withdrawn.

- *Age ineligibility triggers income.* After the end of the year in which you turn 71, repayments to the RRSP can no longer be made because your RRSP is required to have matured by that time. Thus, in the year you turn 71, if there is an outstanding HBP balance, you must repay the outstanding balance or include in income each year the required annual repayment.

- *Disabled persons.* Home Buyers' Plan withdrawals can also be used for the purpose of making home renovations or purchasing a compatible home to meet the needs of a disabled person. For HBP purposes, a disabled person is an individual who qualifies for the disability amount or a person related by blood, marriage, or adoption to a person who is eligible to claim the disability amount for the year of the HBP withdrawal. Disabled persons need not be first-time homebuyers to participate in the HBP.

- *Effect of emigration.* If a HBP participant becomes a non-resident, the outstanding balance must be repaid before the return for the year of emigration is filed and no later than 60 days after becoming a non-resident.

- *Year of death.* In the year of death, the full outstanding amount under the Home Buyers' Plan must be repaid (or included in income) unless, at the time of death, you had a spouse or common-law partner and that individual elects jointly with your legal representative to make the payments under the Home Buyers' Plan. This election may be made in the form of a letter attached to your final return.

Please read Tax Fact #190 now. Note that funds withdrawn under the LLP must be paid back into the RRSP over a 10-year period, beginning in the fifth calendar year after the withdrawal or the year after you cease to be a full-time student for at least three months in the year, whichever comes first. Amounts which are due and not repaid are included in your income in the year they are due.

Here are some additional tax facts:

• *Multiple withdrawals.* You are free to participate in the LLP plan again once you have repaid the amount borrowed.

• *Use of funds.* It is not necessary that you actually use the funds borrowed for the intended purpose, only that you become a full-time student.

• *Use by the disabled.* For LLP purposes, a disabled person is an individual who qualifies for the disability amount for the year of the LLP withdrawal. Disabled persons need not be full-time students to qualify.

• *Emigration.* If an LLP participant becomes a non-resident, the outstanding balance must be repaid before the return for the year of emigration is filed and no later than 60 days after becoming a non-resident.

• *Death.* In the year of death, the full amount outstanding under the Lifelong Learning Plan must be repaid (or included in income) unless, at the time of death, you had a spouse or common-law partner. That survivor could then elect jointly with your legal representative to resume making the payments on a tax exempt basis.

• *Qualifying programs.* A qualifying educational program is an educational program that:
– lasts three consecutive months or more; and
– requires a student to spend 10 hours or more per week on courses or work in the program. Courses or work includes lectures, practical training, and laboratory work, as well as research time spent on a post-graduate thesis. It does not include study time.

Create a tax efficient retirement income

Tired of working but not quite ready to retire? Some employees in this situation are opting for phased retirement. Although the reduced workload can be welcome, the reduced income may present problems. The idea may be to begin receiving a partial pension while continuing to work part time. Follow are some tax-efficient ways to do that:

Tapping into your Company Pension Plan. Did you know that starting in the year 2008, you can continue to work full or part time, while accumulating benefits under a defined benefit register pension plan? Here are the essential tax facts:

- The employee will be able to draw up to 60% of the benefits that have otherwise accrued under the pension plan while continuing to accumulate benefits based on current employment, provided that the employee is at least 55.

- No conditions are imposed on whether the employee works part- or full-time.

- This ability to draw a pension while continuing to accrue benefits will not be extended to designated plans which cover only one employee or a small group of highly compensated individuals.

There is more good news on this front. Consider splitting the income you receive from qualifying superannuation benefits with your spouse. That way, you could earn taxable income from employment sources, while transferring your tax liability on up to 50% of qualifying pension income to your spouse. This opens up a second pension income amount of up to $2000.

You should then consider maximizing your opportunities under the Attribution Rules. That is, invest your employment earnings to create new funds in non-registered savings accounts; spend the pension received in your spouse's hands, as investments of those funds will result in attribution of the investment earnings back to you.

Tapping into your RRSP. Well, imagine: you have spent much of your life accumulating money in your RRSP and now it is time to spend it! When you becomes age-ineligible (the end of the year in which you turn 71), run out of contribution room, or when it is simply time to start a pension benefit, there are several options to choose from for creating income.

The RRSP accumulations can be taken out in a lump sum (not usually a good idea as the amounts will be taxed at the highest marginal rate at that time) or you can choose to space out your withdrawals periodically. Note that the new pension income splitting rules are not as advantageous for RRSP holders, who must wait longer to take advantage of them. That is, they must be age 65 to qualify for the pension income amount (or receiving the amounts as a result of the spouse's death).

Withdrawals from an RRSP will be reported on a T4RSP slip, recorded as income on Line 115 if they represent a periodic pension withdrawal or otherwise, Line 129. Withdrawals will be subject to withholding tax at the following rates:

Up to $5,000	10%
$5,000 to $15,000	20%
Above $15,000	30%

Especially when you take a lump sum from your RRSP, it is important for you to take this withholding tax into consideration before you make a withdrawal, to ensure you end up with the exact amount of funds you need for the purpose you have in mind. Withholdings can be minimized by taking several smaller withdrawals, rather than one large one.

Withdrawals of Undeducted Amounts and Overcontributions. Sometimes you'll want to withdraw money from an RRSP because you have undeducted contributions, or over-contributions. Such withdrawals are not taxable.

RRSP over-contributions. Overcontributions often happen when when you instruct your employer to make RRSP contributions on your behalf through a payroll deduction plan, but forget to tell him about a change in your contribution room due to a tax reassessment.

Essential TAX FACT #191

Stay away from making "excess contributions". These are RRSP contributions which exceed your contribution room plus $2,000.

To cushion errors in contributions due to fluctuating RRSP room, an overcontribution limit of $2,000 is allowed without penalty, provided you are at least 18 in the preceding taxation year. Many taxpayers, in fact, use that rule for tax planning purposes: it's a great way to make even more tax deferred income within your RRSP.

Debbie for example, has RRSP contribution room of $5,000, which she has contributed. But she is allowed to contribute a total of $7,000 without penalty, and decides to do so to earn tax deferred investment income while the money is in the plan.

Also note the following in managing your RRSP withdrawals:

- *Withdrawal of undeducted contributions.* Amounts contributed to your RRSP and not yet deducted may be withdrawn tax-free and with no withholding taxes by filing *Form T3012A, Tax Deduction Waiver on the Refund of Your Undeducted RRSP Contributions.* The amount withdrawn will be included on a T4RSP slip and must be reported as income. You may, however, claim an offsetting deduction on your tax return. Taxpayers who withdraw undeducted contributions without using *Form T3012A* will have tax withheld but may use *Form T746* to calculate their allowable deduction on line 232.

- *Contributions in excess of overcontribution limits.* Excess RRSP contributions are subject to a penalty tax of 1% per month. A complicated form called a *T1-OVP* must be completed in that case and the penalty must be paid by March 31 of the year following. Penalties will accrue until the excess contributions are withdrawn from the RRSP. You'll want to ask a professional to help you with this form.

- *Special rule for minors.* Taxpayers who were at least 18 in the prior taxation year may contribute the full amount of their contribution room plus a $2,000 overcontribution. Overcontributions are not allowed for taxpayers who are minors.

Tax Free Transfers to an RRSP. The following capital sources may be transferred to your RRSP on a tax free basis over and above the normal RRSP contribution limits plus the $2,000 allowable overcontribution:

- *Eligible retiring allowances.* Amounts received on job termination as a severance package may be rolled over into an RRSP on a tax free basis depending on certain conditions. *For service after 1995*, no RRSP rollover is allowed. *For service after 1988 and before 1996*, a single limit of $2,000 per year of service can be rolled into an RRSP. And *for service before 1989*, it is possible to roll over $2,000 for each year of service plus another $1,500 for each year in which the employer's contributions to the company pension plan did not vest in you. The eligible amount will be shown on the T4A from the former employer. In applying these rules, a single day in a calendar year counts as a "year" of employment.

- *Funds from another RRSP.* You may request a direct transfer of RRSP accumulations from one RRSP to another RRSP under which you are the annuitant. *Form T2033* may be used to effect the transfer.

- *Funds from a spouse's RRSP.* On the breakdown of a marriage or common-law relationship, where the terms of a separation or divorce agreement require that the funds from one spouse's RRSP be transferred to the other, the funds may be transferred tax free. *Form T2220* must be used.

- *RPP amounts.* If you cease to belong to an RPP, the funds from the RPP may be transferred to your RRSP. *Form T2151* must be used.

- *DPSP accumulations.* You may transfer funds from your DPSP to your RRSP. *Form T2151* must be used.

- *Foreign pension receipts.* Lump sum amounts received from a foreign pension plan in respect of a period while you were a non-resident may be transferred to your RRSP. Amounts that are exempt from tax under a tax treaty with the foreign country may not be transferred.

- *Saskatchewan pension plan amounts.* A lump sum payment out of the Saskatchewan pension plan may be transferred to your RRSP tax free.

Tax Free Transfers from an RRSP. Funds from your RRSP may be transferred on a tax free basis to:

- A *Registered Pension Plan* (only possible if the RPP terms allow this). *Form T2033* may be used.

- *Another RRSP.*

- *The RRSP of a spouse or former spouse on breakdown of marriage or common-law relationship.*

- *A RRIF.* You may transfer funds from your RRSP to a RRIF under which you are the annuitant. *Form T2033* must be used.

- *The RRIF of a spouse or former spouse on breakdown of marriage or common-law relationship. Form T2220* must be used.

- *An annuity.* Amounts can be transferred from your RRSP to an annuity contract for your life or jointly for the life of you and your spouse or common-law partner with or without a guarantee period. If there is a guarantee period, it may not be for a period longer than until you (or spouse or common-law partner) are 90 years old.

- *RRSP of spouse or former spouse or dependant on death.*

Creating your Pension. When it comes time to create your periodic pension withdrawals from an RRSP, the accumulations will generally be transferred into one of two investment vehicles that will enable a periodic taxable income:

- *an annuity* (which provides for equal monthly payments over a period of time)

- *a Registered Retirement Income Funds (RRIF)*, which provides for gradually increasing payments over time.

Under a RRIF, a minimum amount must be withdrawn according to a pre-determined chart, under which payments increase over time. The payments are taxable in the year received. However you can withdraw more than this as required.

As with RRSP payments, the amounts will qualify for the $2,000 pension income amount on Line 314 if you are over age 64 or receiving the amounts as the result of a spouse's death.

Before you withdraw, speak to your tax advisors about planning your income sources, taking into account the following concepts:

- Equalizing income between spouses—who should withdraw first or most—the higher income earner or the lower?

- Can other income sources be split between spouses—Canada Pension Plan benefits for example?

- Should dividends be transferred from the lower earner to the higher earner (a possibility only if a Spousal Amount is thereby created or increased)?

- Should one spouse be earning more or less interest, dividends or capital gains from non-registered sources to reduce family net income?

- How will the clawback of the Age Amount or Old Age Security be affected by your pension withdrawals?

- How will your quarterly instalment payments be affected by your RRSP withdrawals?

- If you will be in a higher marginal tax bracket at death, should you withdraw more during your lifetime?

For information about RRSP accumulations at death, see Part Five.

Plan to split income in retirement

With our progressive tax system, the more evenly you can spread your household income amongst family members, the more likely it is that you'll pay the least amount of income tax as a family. During the earning years, the opportunities for splitting earned income are severely limited, but several opportunities exist to split retirement income and thereby reduce your total tax bill. We have discussed some of these opportunities already; let's explore further:

Spousal RRSPs have been available for some time. When one spouse has higher earned income than the other, the spousal RRSP provides an opportunity for both the self-employed and those who will not be receiving a pension income to split RRSP income in retirement with their spouse. The spouse with the higher earned income claims the RRSP deduction thereby reducing their income tax bill but the spouse (in whose name the contribution is made) will report the RRSP income when it is withdrawn as retirement income.

Where the spouses are different ages, use of a spousal plan can defer the time when the plan must be matured and a retirement income is taken until the year that spouse turns 71. A spousal plan can therefore provide a longer tax-free accumulation period than would otherwise be available.

Splitting of Canada Pension Plan benefits is beneficial if one spouse receives significantly more CPP benefits than the other. Through a simple application to Human Resources Development Canada, CPP benefits earned while the couple was together may be split between them.

Splitting of other pension income became possible in 2007. Under new rules, spouses or common-law partners may elect to each report a portion of "eligible" pension income received. Essentially this is income that qualifies for the $2,000 pension income amount. Up to one-half of such pension income received can be reported by the recipient's spouse. Splitting of pension income between spouses can be beneficial but not for all taxpayers.

The following should be taken into account when planning for splitting of retirement income:

- the effect on the Age Amount and OAS clawback on both the transferor and the transferee;

- the effect on total non-refundable credits available to the family unit, considering specifically the Age Amount, the Pension Amount, the Spousal Amount and credits transferable;

- the potential for moving the transferor to a lower bracket and the impact of potentially moving the transferee to a higher bracket.

Example 1: One spouse with high income

George has $100,000 of eligible pension income and $200,000 of interest income. Betty receives only the Old Age Pension.

If George and Betty elect to transfer half of his eligible pension income—$50,000—to her return, the following are the results:

- Betty's age amount is reduced from the maximum of $5,276 to $1,592.

- George loses the ability to claim a spousal amount credit of $3,518.

- Betty is able to claim the pension amount of $2,000. Betty's OAS is not clawed back.

- *Total federal tax is reduced by $5,726.*

The benefit enjoyed by accessing Betty's lower tax rates more than offsets the value of the credits forgone.

Example 2: Both spouses have income

Jim and David are common-law partners. Jim receives the OAS, has $60,000 of eligible pension income and $30,000 of interest income. David receives only the Old Age Pension and has $20,000 of interest income.

If Jim and David elect to transfer half of his eligible pension income—$30,000, the following are the results:

- David's age amount is reduced from the maximum of $5,276 to $1,592.

- Jim's OAS clawback is reduced by $4,500.

- David is able to claim the pension amount of $2,000.

- David's OAS is not clawed back.

- *Total federal tax is reduced by $461, but there is a reduction in OAS clawback of $4,500 for a total saving of $4,961.*

The tax rate saving on moving the income to David's return is almost the same as the net tax credits lost. The reduction in Jim's OAS clawback provides most of the saving.

Example 3: Lower Income Spouses

Lynn and Henry are married. Lynn receives the OAS, has $15,000 of eligible pension income and $20,000 of interest income. Henry receives only the Old Age Pension. If Lynn and Henry elect to transfer half of her eligible pension income—$7,500, the following are the results:

- Lynn's age amount clawback is reduced by $1,125.
- Lynn loses her spousal claim for Henry of $3,518.
- Henry's transfer of unused credits to Lynn is reduced by $3,982.
- Henry is able to claim the $2,000 pension amount credit.
- *Total federal tax is reduced by $224.*

Although total personal credits available following the transfer are actually less than they were before the transfer, overall tax is reduced, because before the transfer Lynn had some income taxed in the second bracket; now all income is taxed in the lowest bracket.

Therefore, it is important to have a qualified tax professional assist you with the tax calculations to determine exactly whether pension income splitting is of benefit to you. It can make thousands of dollars difference over your golden years.

Planning a Pension for RDSP Beneficiaries. A disabled person who is a beneficiary of an RDSP must begin to take benefits from it in the year he or she turns 60. Those benefits will not affect any other means-tested support delivered through the income tax system including the OAS.

Each payment made from a RDSP is considered to be comprised of grants, bonds and investment income and each such part is included in the beneficiary's income when received effective the 2008 and subsequent tax years.

There in an ***annual limit*** on the amount paid equal to the value of the assets of the plan at the beginning of the year divided by a factor equal to three plus the remaining number of years the beneficiary is expected to live ("life expectancy") as determined by Statistics Canada. Such information is available on the CRA website.

Exceptions to these rules will be allowed when the beneficiary has survived beyond the normal life expectancy. In that case the limit on payments to be made will be one-third of the value of the plan's assets at the beginning of the year.

The second exception occurs when the director of the plan provides written certification from a medical doctor that shows the beneficiary's life expectancy to be shorter than otherwise determined, in which case the calculation is based on the age to which the beneficiary can be expected to live.

Payments from an RDSP can be one of three types:

- a disability assistance payment made to the beneficiary or the beneficiary's estate,

- a transfer to another RDSP or

- a repayment that is required to be made to the government.

It may be a good idea to receive assistance from a tax and legal advisor in planning these payments to ensure all other tax preferences and social benefits available to the disabled taxpayer can be maximized.

Preparing for death and widowhood

No personal financial plan can be completed without a plan for transferring assets to the next generation, yet the majority of Canadians are reluctant to discuss the transfer of their assets with family members and many don't have a will. But to paraphrase Benjamin Franklin, death and taxes are perhaps the only two constants we can count on from the moment of birth… and it pays well to be prepared for the inevitable.

Essential TAX FACT #192

Wealth can be effectively passed along to others during your lifetime or upon your demise. But what's important is that you begin immediately to set up an estate plan with your financial advisors and that you have a will.

A lifetime of complicated personal relationships makes that more difficult, especially if you are wealthy. Whether you are already alone or preparing to be alone, protecting your assets at the time of death is an important obligation to your family as well as society. Consider the following checklist for starting an estate plan:

Objectives for starting an estate plan

- *Identify financial institutions.* where are your assets held? Include key contacts.

- *Identify advisors.* Who are your professional advisors including banker, accountant, lawyer, stockbroker, insurance agent and what is their contact info?

Essential TAX FACT #193

Singles may choose as their heirs a favorite charity, particularly if there are no other related or non-related parties to whom assets will be transferred. Charitable giving requires planning as well, and there are numerous generous provisions available through the tax system.

Essential TAX FACT #194

Your total charitable gifts for the year cannot exceed 75% of your net income on Line 236, except in the year of death, when it can equal 100% of your net income. Donations may be in the form of money or capital property.

Essential TAX FACT #195

If you give capital property to charity, your donation limit is increased by 25% of any CCA recapture or capital gains arising on the donation.

- *Identify proxies.* Who will exercise Power of Attorney if you become disabled or cannot direct your own personal affairs?

- *Identify heirs.* List exact contact information, as well as their relationship to you. In the case of singles, these heirs could include your favorite charity. Discuss options for the transfer of assets and funds during your lifetime and at death.

- *Identify gifts.* Sketch out what you wish for each of your heirs to receive.

- *Identify needs.* Will any of your heirs require assistance with ongoing income?

- *Identify executors.* Prepare a list of possible executor(s) and make approaches.

- *Identify guardians.* Prepare a list of those to whom you would trust the care of your minor children, as well as those who should not have that responsibility.

- *Identify business succession plans.* How should your business interests be distributed, and who should step in to run the show?

- *Plan for probate fees and capital gains taxes at death.* Review life insurance policies that may be used for those purposes.

- *Identify capital assets* and their fair market value annually.

- *Identify asset transfer instructions.* Which assets should be transferred during your lifetime, and which should be transferred only upon your death?

- *Make plans for safekeeping.* Keep all important documents in a safety deposit box and identify the location.

- *Deal with debt.* Cleaning up spilled milk is no fun for anyone…especially if it's been there for awhile. List debt obligations and the order they should be repaid. Make a list of on-going financial obligations that should be cancelled on death.
- *Draw up your will.* Tell your lawyer where it is to be kept.

Filing consequences at time of death. When you die, one mandatory final return must filed for the period January 1 to date of death, and this return must be filed by the later of:

- April 30 of the year immediately following the year of death
- six months after date of death

See Tax Fact 197. Note, however, the final return from January to date of death is usually the only one most taxpayers will file. On that return, income earned up to date of death is reported. Certain income sources must be "prorated" to the date of death, including employment earnings, pension receipts, interest, rents, royalties, or annuity income. Offsetting expenses are accrued to date of death in a similar fashion.

When you die, you are deemed to have disposed of your assets immediately before death, usually at Fair Market Value (FMV). However, the value of the deemed disposition can vary, depending on who will acquire the assets… your spouse (including common-law partner), child or another. Transfers to children or others are generally made at the property's FMV; transfers to spouse can be at the asset's adjusted cost base (or UCC in the case of depreciable assets) or FMV.

Essential TAX FACT #196

A special tax break is allowed when publicly traded mutual funds, shares, stock options, bonds, bills, warrants or futures listed on a prescribed stock exchange are donated to charity: for donations before May 2, 2006, the income inclusion on disposition of these assets will be one half the normal capital gains inclusion rates. For donations after May 1, the capital gains inclusion rate is zero. You get a charitable donation credit for the full value of the donation but do not have to pay any taxes on the increase in value of the shares. Complete *Form T1170 Capital Gains on Gifts of Certain Capital Property.*

Essential TAX FACT #197

There are several "elective returns" that can be filed on death, which will allow you to claim again certain personal amounts, to result in a substantial tax benefit.

Essential TAX FACT #198

The most significant transaction on the final return could revolve around the disposition of capital assets. That's because a deemed disposition of your assets is considered to have taken place immediately before your death.

Essential TAX FACT #199

If you transfer capital property to your spouse during your lifetime, resulting capital gains or losses on disposition are taxed back in your hands, unless your spouse pays fair value, as discussed in earlier chapters. In general, no disposition will be considered to have taken place at fair market value at that time, unless you so elect.

Essential TAX FACT #200

Be sure to provide your executor with a copy of the 1994 tax return and in particular *Form T664* upon which a capital gains election may have been made to use up your $100,000 Capital Gains Exemption. This will affect the calculation of the deemed disposition of capital properties on the final return.

The use of "tax-free rollovers". The deemed disposition rules on death of the taxpayer therefore override the Attribution Rules that apply while living. That is, capital property transferred to the spouse on your death will not be taxed until your spouse disposes of the property. The spouse will use your adjusted cost base, and pay tax on the full gain from the time you acquired the asset, thereby completely postponing the tax consequences at the time of your death until your spouse dies or sells the property.

Depending on your taxable income at the time of your death, your executor may wish to roll over assets to the spouse on a tax free basis, or have them transfer at fair market value. Fair value may make sense if you have unused capital losses from the past that have been carried forward. Such balances can often be used to offset income created by the higher valuations that have accrued to the date of death. It will also provide your survivors with the opportunity to start with a higher adjusted cost base on the acquisition of your assets, which will save them money down the line as well.

In the absence of those plans, capital gains or losses resulting from the deemed disposition of your assets on death must be reported, together with any recapture or terminal loss on depreciable assets, with the resulting tax payable (if any) on that return.

RRSPs and Other Pensions. Didn't spend it all? What happens when you die and leave unspent accumulations in your RRSP?

You are deemed to have received the fair market value of all assets in your RRSP or RRIF immediately prior to death. If there is a surviving spouse or common-law partner the assets may be transferred tax-free to that person's registered plan (RRSP or RRIF). Similar provisions allow for the transfer of Deferred Profit Sharing Plans and Registered Pension Plan. In certain circumstances, the RRSP can be transferred to a financially dependent child or grandchild, even when there is a surviving spouse. Speak to your tax advisors about these options.

Essential TAX FACT #201

Request a clearance certificate from CRA to relieve the executor of any further liability.

Essential TAX FACT #202

Try not to make major financial or lifestyle changes within one year after the death of a spouse.

Tax-Free Savings Plans. Accumulated earnings in your TFSA are not taxable, but earning after death no longer accumulate tax free. However the assets may be rolled over to the TFSA of a surviving spouse or common-law partner.

CHAPTER REFLECTION:
ESSENTIAL TAX FACTS FOR WEALTH PRESERVATION

1. One of the reasons why today's Canadians are wealthier than generations before is that their financial assets include real estate and private pension accumulations.

2. You may wish to think of your capital accumulations within three primary categories:
   a. Tax exempt assets
   b. Tax prepaid assets
   c. Tax-assisted accumulations

3. When you withdraw money from an RRSP, both principal and earnings must be added in full to your taxable income, in the year of withdrawal, unless you withdraw under a Home Buyers' Plan or a Lifelong Learning Plan.

4. You can use the tax system to create new capital without coming up with any new money, by "flipping" assets held in a non-registered account into an RRSP, thereby creating new tax savings.

5. The increase in value in capital assets held outside registered accounts will accrue on a tax-deferred basis until they are disposed of. Then, only 50% of the gains are taxable.

6. You might even own some tax exempt assets…for most households that includes one tax exempt principal residence.

7. Sometimes assets are sold to strangers or transferred to relatives. In fact, often assets can be transferred to spouses or children without immediate tax consequences.

8. You can dispose of your assets through an actual sale or on a deemed disposition.

9. When you transfer assets to your adult children during your lifetime, the property is always transferred at fair market value and tax consequences are immediately reported.

10. Capital losses may only be used to reduce capital gains in the current year. If losses exceed gains, they may be carried back to reduce capital gains in any of the previous three years or in any subsequent year.

11. Gains on the disposition of personal use property are taxable, but subject to the "The $1,000 Rule".

12. In most cases, capital gains on disposition of the principal residence will be exempt from tax.

13. When a principal residence is used in part for business purposes (home office, child care enterprises, consulting, etc.) it is possible to retain the principal residence exemption as long as no capital cost allowance is claimed on the property.

14. When an income-producing building is acquired, special reporting rules must be followed.

15. When real estate is disposed of, the proceeds must be allocated to the land and building as well as other depreciable property.

16. On deciding whether a transaction is "income" or "capital" in nature, the courts have considered a list of individual circumstances.

17. It is CRA's view that the subdivision of farmland or inherited land in order to sell it will not necessarily constitute a conversion to inventory.

18. When you trade some of a group of identical shares, you must calculate the new average cost each time there is a purchase.

19. Should a disposition of a qualified small business corporation share result in a capital gain, a lifetime capital gains exemption of $750,000 may be available.

20. Interest deductibility will hinge upon the direct and current use of money borrowed and the identification of an income-producing purpose.

21. Opportunities exist for splitting retirement income through spousal RRSPs, actual splitting of CPP benfits, or electing to split reporting of pension income.

STAY CURRENT—WHAT'S NEW?

Beginning in 2008, employees may begin receiving partial pension benefits under an RPP while continuing to contribute to that or another RPP.

Tax-Free Savings Accounts, new for 2009 will, over time, become an important tool in accumulating wealth for many taxpayers, especially those who are not eligible to contribute to an RRSP.

NOW PUT MORE MONEY IN YOUR POCKET ALL YEAR LONG...

PERSPECTIVE

We hope that we have accomplished our mission in writing this book: to show you hundreds of simple ways to put more money in your pocket at tax time—and all year long. We hope that you will be motivated to take control of your after-tax results and learn even more. The checklist below might help you develop a script to start this discussion with your professional financial advisors:

☐ Review personal financial statements: net worth, cash flow, budget, bank reconciliation, balance sheets and income and expense statements.

☐ Take stock of RRSP Contribution Room: contribute to your RRSP regularly.

- [ ] Set up and make regular contributions to your Tax-Free Savings Account.

- [ ] Acquire a tax-exempt personal residence.

- [ ] Maximize earnings from non-registered savings by keeping an eagle eye on after-tax returns.

- [ ] Accumulate capital.

- [ ] Choose your mate with care. Mistakes here can really set you back. Plan for the end of your relationship while you still like each other.

- [ ] Be ready for family. Be emotionally and financially secure enough to do a great job raising your children. Don't let them down—they are the future.

- [ ] Have the right kind of insurance. Protect yourself, your family and your business from calamities beyond your control.

- [ ] Have a will. No matter how young you are, plan for your demise along the way to capture the full power of your productivity. Update annually at tax filing time.

- [ ] Stay current: keep on top of the changing tax rules throughout your lifetime.

- [ ] Be aware of lifecycle change. Revisit your goals during times of change.

- [ ] Embrace lifelong learning: seek educational opportunities that result in new thinking, analytical skills as well as "hands on" experiences.

- [ ] But… you can't know everything: enlist the help of a professional team dedicated to your goals.

Essential TAX FACT #203

Managing your money will be a lifelong affair. Keeping on top of your right to arrange your affairs within the framework of the law to pay only the correct amount of tax—and not one cent more—will enhance the process. But, in the end, remember that your money is only a tool that will help you in your quest for self-actualization.

INDEX

EDUCATION OPPORTUNITIES
ONLY FROM

Knowledge Bureau
CANADA'S LEADING EDUCATOR IN TAX AND FINANCIAL SERVICES

About The Knowledge Bureau

The Knowledge Bureau is a national certified educational institute which provides continuing professional development to practicing professionals in tax and financial services leading to certification and designation. We are the home of the Distinguished Financial Advisor (DFA) and Master Financial Advisor (MFA) designations.

For an information brochure on self study programs, workshops, webcasts and private client in-company programs, see contact information below.

The Knowledge Bureau is also the publishing home to a new series of strategic planning books for concerned investors and their advisors entitled the *Master Your Personal Finances Series: Financial Education for Decision Makers.* Titles launching in early 2009 include *Master Your Real Wealth*, *Master Your Retirement*, and *Master Your Money Management*.

Other titles by Evelyn Jacks
Make Sure It's Deductible
Master Your Taxes

By Evelyn Jacks and Jean Blacklock
Get Your People To Work Like They Mean It!

For more information contact The Knowledge Bureau at **1-866-953-4769** or by email: **reception@knowledgebureau.com,** or visit **www.knowledgebureau.com.**

Designation Programs from
The Knowledge Bureau 2009

The DFA (Distinguished Financial Advisor)

Program 1: Tax Services Specialist

Tax preparers, planners and advisors need to know the details of continuous tax change, using expert professional tax software and research skills. Taxpayers who want to take control of their planning activities or better guide their financial advisors may also be candidates for this program, featuring the most current information on tax compliance, tax planning, budget proposals and jurisprudence. Six courses are required for designation (courses may also be taken individually for certification and accreditation):

- ☐ STP0107   Introduction to Computer-Based Personal Tax Preparation
- ☐ STP0407   Advanced Tax Preparation and Research
- ☐ STP0607   Tax Preparation for Proprietorships
- ☐ SBP0108   Basic Bookkeeping for Business
- ☐ STP0508   Introduction to Corporate Tax Preparation
- ☐ SEP0203   Death of a Taxpayer

Or substitute up to two of the above with:

- ☐ SFP0408   Cross Border Taxation
- ☐ SEP0308   Use of Trusts in Tax and Estate Planning

Program 2: Certified Bookkeeping Specialist

Bookkeepers must be tax-compliant data managers who assist business owners with proper and timely information as front-line stewards of financial resources throughout the lifecycle of a business. By earning your DFA as Certified Bookkeeping Specialist, you'll maximize your value proposition to your family business, your clients and their advisors with the skills to facilitate planning for the employee, investor and owner-manager. Six courses are required for designation (courses may also be taken individually for certification and accreditation):

- ☐ SBP0108   Basic Bookkeeping for Business
- ☐ SBP0206   Managerial Accounting for Professional Bookkeepers
- ☐ SBP0506   Advanced Bookkeeping for a Selection of Business Profiles
- ☐ SBP0606   Advanced Payroll for Professional Bookkeepers
- ☐ SBP0406   Advanced Business Issues for Professional Advisors
- ☐ SBP0706   Tax Planning for the Corporate Owner-Manager

Or substitute up to two of the above with:

- ☐ STP0107   Introduction to Computer-Based Personal Tax Preparation
- ☐ STP0508   Introduction to Corporate Tax Preparation

Consult our website for more information: **www.knowledgebureau.com**

The MFA (Master Financial Advisor)

Program 1: Retirement Income Specialist

Investment advisors who wish to meet the demand for tax-efficient income and real wealth management as their clients transition from accumulation to spending for wants and needs in retirement will welcome the opportunity to study this leading edge program. It is designed to provide structure and process for developing and monitoring tax efficient retirement income plans featuring tax efficient planning software. It covers a holistic retirement income planning process and consistent income-producing solutions. Six courses are required for designation (courses may also be taken individually for certification and accreditation):

- ☐ SRP0507   Tax-Efficient Retirement Income Planning
- ☐ SFP0207   Financial Literacy: The Relationship Between Risk and Return
- ☐ SIP0607   Portfolio Construction for Real Wealth Management
- ☐ SFP0308   Advising Family Businesses
- ☐ SBP0706   Tax Planning for the Corporate Owner-Manager
- ☐ SEP0308   Use of Trusts in Tax and Estate Planning

Or substitute up to two of the above with:
- ☐ SIS0106   Insurance Strategies for the Small Business Owner
- ☐ SEP0203   Death of a Taxpayer

Program 2: Investment Planning Services Specialist

Learn the skills of real wealth management related to investment income planning. This program is designed to provide structure and process for advisors interested in specializing in tax efficient Investment Planning Services planning. It covers a holistic Investment Planning Services planning process and consistent income-producing solutions. Six courses are required for designation (courses may also be taken individually for certification and accreditation):

- ☐ SFP0103   Client-Centred Practices
- ☐ SFP0207   Financial Literacy: The Relationship Between Risk and Return
- ☐ SIP0506   Portfolio Risk Manager
- ☐ SFP0408   Cross Border Taxation
- ☐ SIP0708   Elements of Real Wealth Management
- ☐ SIP0808   Tax Efficient Investment Income Planning

Or substitute up to two of the above with:
- ☐ STP0205   Tax Planning for the Small Business Owner
- ☐ SIS0403   Life Insurance: Strategic Investment Planning with Universal Life
- ☐ SIP0607   Portfolio Construction for Real Wealth Management

Program 3: Certificate of Achievement in Personal Finance

For your personal self improvement and financial literacy. The Knowledge Bureau has chosen 8 of its professional certificate courses which may be of interest to laypeople who want to learn more about tax and financial services in order to have a better relationship with their advisors or to learn to do some of the planning themselves. Any six courses in the program will lead to the Certificate of Achievement in Personal Finance.

- ☐ SRP0507   Tax-Efficient Retirement Income Planning
- ☐ STP0107   Introduction to Computer-Based Personal Tax Preparation
- ☐ SBP0108   Basic Bookkeeping for Business
- ☐ STP0205   Tax Planning for the Small Business Owner
- ☐ SEP0203   Death of a Taxpayer
- ☐ SEP0308   Use of Trusts in Tax and Estate Planning

Or substitute up to two of the above with:
- ☐ SFP0207   Financial Literacy: The Relationship Between Risk and Return
- ☐ SIS0303   Medical Perspective on Elder Care

Knowledge Bureau
CANADA'S LEADING EDUCATOR IN TAX AND FINANCIAL SERVICES

The Knowledge Bureau, publisher of the annual favorite, Evelyn Jacks' *Essential Tax Facts*, is proud to present its **NEW** expanded line of Newsbooks 2009: *Master Your Personal Finances: Financial Education for Decision Makers*.

In turbulent times, everyday Canadians are looking for sound answers to their personal finance questions. They want
- to take control
- get better results from their investments
- improve predictability of their outcomes
- to retire with dignity, gracefully and with enough money
- address worries about stewardship of their money and their kids' values
- understand global investing and associated volatility
- get a handle on their taxes
- address concerns about their ability to saving, credit and debt
- have more profitable relationships with their advisors

This comes at a time when new readers are interested in personal finance for the first time:
- financial literacy is a concern in North America and around the globe
- women, who for the first time are entering retirement with their own pensions and capital assets
- seniors, who are living longer, are wealthier but are vulnerable
- highly educated young adults who have the potential for great wealth, but do not understand basic financial strategies
- the emerging middle class—immigrants in North America, but in addition the new baby boom in India, China, Asia—who are internet savvy.

The Knowledge Bureau is proud to present the **Master Yours Series** of books to address these concerns. Less a "how to" than a "strategic planning" book, each one will give the reader the facts:
- real life scenarios you may find yourself in
- the issues: what you need to know
- the solutions: how you can get help and take control
- the tips and traps: how to master your money and gain peace of mind

Powerful. Masterful. This line talks to up, not down to its audience…a critical element in capturing the confidence of a new generation of personal finance readers: women, the young, the emerging wealth and of course, your traditional readers.

Knowledge Bureau Education Services

Toll Free: 1 866 953-4769 Web: www.knowledgebureau.com